Teaching
by Heart

Teaching by Heart

One Professor's Journey to Inspire

THOMAS J. DeLONG

Harvard Business Review Press

Boston, Massachusetts

The web addresses referenced in this book were live and correct at the time of the book's publication but may be subject to change.

Library of Congress Cataloging-in-Publication Data

Names: DeLong, Thomas, author.
Title: Teaching by heart : one professor's journey to inspire / Thomas J. DeLong.
Description: Boston : Harvard Business Review Press, [2019] | Includes index.
Identifiers: LCCN 2019031069 | ISBN 9781633698529 (hardcover)
Subjects: LCSH: Teaching. | Leadership. | Teachers—Attitudes. | Instructional
    systems—Design.
Classification: LCC LB1025.3 .D484 2019 | DDC 371.102—dc23
LC record available at https://lccn.loc.gov/2019031069

ISBN: 978-1-63369-852-9
eISBN: 978-1-63369-853-6

The paper used in this publication meets the requirements of the American National Standard for Permanence of Paper for Publications and Documents in Libraries and Archives Z39.48-1992.

To Raji and M. K. Vijayaraghavan
Through you I've experienced unconditional love

CONTENTS

Teaching
by Heart

Introduction

After a recent World Cup, I heard a member of the Brazilian team lament, "We never felt the shirt." The expression suggests a lack of engagement and passion, and from the moment I could differentiate between a mesmerizing teacher and a passionless teacher, I knew which teacher was "feeling the shirt." In seventh grade, I couldn't take my eyes off Mr. Walter Stickel as he told story after story about Lewis and Clark trudging up the Columbia River in a rainstorm, chilled to the bone.

It was then that I became a student of great teaching. This book attempts to unpack what I've experienced, studied, and observed over the past fifty-two years regarding teachers—to convey how in their best moments, they can lift people up, and in their worst, let them down.

At times, I'm also going to draw parallels between teaching and leadership. While these are two distinct activities, my experiences as a Harvard Business School professor and as a corporate leader have demonstrated that these two disciplines are inextricably intertwined. More to the point, I've found that the best teachers are also leaders, and the best leaders are also teachers. For this reason, I will occasionally discuss both in concert, especially the lessons teachers can learn from leaders and managers.

I will take you inside great institutions—Harvard being the first and foremost of them—attempting to impart how to lead and teach. I will also take you inside my own head and heart. I've "felt the shirt" as teacher and leader, and on occasion have misplaced my shirt somewhere between home and work.

I've experienced the highs and the lows. In terms of the latter, I read a teacher evaluation form on which one student wrote she was frightened to come to my class, fearing that I would make fun of her. I never did, but my humor frightened her. Though I'm not intending to make my students fearful, that was the effect in this case. When I read this evaluation, I felt shame and guilt and remorse and self-pity all wrapped in a messy emotional package. I've also received a letter from a former student expressing how his life was transformed through my teaching; the letter brought tears of joy. The positive feelings dissipate quickly, though, and the negative ones linger.

As teachers, we focus more on our inadequacies and failures than on our strengths and accomplishments. I'll deconstruct why this is so. I will walk you through the heaven and hell of teaching by dissecting and analyzing what I've experienced in the Harvard Business School classroom.

Yes, the Harvard classroom is different. But it's also the same. Harvard is an elite institution, light years removed from a junior college classroom. But I've found that a classroom is a classroom, no matter the institution that houses it or the age level of its students. I've taught in Utah, in corporations, and in various venues globally. Though I'm going to focus primarily on Harvard Business School, the vast majority of the teaching experiences I describe are universal.

I hope to take you on an adventure where, at the end of the experience, you will be better able to develop a sense of what makes a great teacher and pick up lessons about how to teach and lead better. I know this is an ambitious objective—you may be wondering if this is a book about teaching or a psychological study. But as you'll discover, understanding your patterns of behaviors is crucial to any discussion about teaching. You need to ask yourself: What is it that I do consistently that assists me living and teaching, that leverages my talents in unique ways? Just as important, you need to understand those emotional or behavioral patterns that sabotage your efforts to make a difference.

I'll discuss what needs to be done to disrupt those patterns so that you can experience the present without being encumbered by your past or by the fears you have of the future.

I'll also delve into the mysteries and occasional miracles of teaching. For instance, how does a teacher enter a state of being where she feels "flow" for eighty minutes, creating magic by stringing a series of one-act plays together during the class session?

We'll spend a lot of time inside the classrooms of Harvard Business School, where I've taught for the past twenty years. I will deconstruct the process of creating a curriculum and preparing for an eighty-minute class, describing the nerve-wracking fifteen minutes before class begins and the intricate, idiosyncratic nature of the teaching experience. Along the way, I'll step back and connect specific classroom behaviors with leadership issues—in organizations, teams, and one's own life.

And I'll ask—and answer—some provocative questions:

- What happens on multiple levels while teaching? What am I thinking and feeling while at the same time trying to process what the students are thinking and feeling?

- How are my internal conversations affecting how I teach? What are the students' internal dialogues revolving around? Are they in the classroom or somewhere else?

- How might I pull them back into the moment, so they are having an intimate, personal experience with seventy-nine other students?

- What am I thinking and feeling in those reflective moments after a class has ended?

- How can I manage my emotions, review what transpired in the classroom, write down notes on how I'll connect today's lesson with tomorrow's lesson, and evaluate the performance of my students?

- As I gaze out the window of my office, what am I conjuring in my head? Are my thoughts and emotions constructive, destructive, numbing?

And there are other teaching questions worth addressing that relate to being on the faculty of a leading academic institution, including the following:

- How do faculty teach one another?

- How do faculty members use the culture to find their way and create a great career in academia?

- How do faculty members get in their own way and sabotage their own efforts by working against one another?

Through this journey, I will discuss my own patterns—habits of the heart and of the mind that were formed early and have played out throughout my life. These patterns include experiencing life in extremes, rocketing between the polarities of great highs and low lows. As I've become more attuned to these patterns, my students, my children, and I have reaped the benefits. Teachers need to be aware of their patterns in order to manage them.

Without this awareness, they will leave a classroom feeling like I did—either the best teacher or the worst. When I felt like the latter, I caused undue pain for those around me as well as for myself.

As you may have already figured out, I'm going to use myself as a case study throughout this book. As embarrassing as it may be at times to reveal my doubts and neuroses, not to mention my mistakes and failures, I don't see how I can deconstruct teaching without deconstructing the teacher I know best. While I'll occasionally cite other books and conceptual frameworks, this book isn't designed to be an academically rigorous analysis of teaching. It's personal, and so I'm going to share a lot of stories about myself and other teachers whom I know or have observed.

Over the years, I've learned a lot both theoretically and practically about teaching. For instance, I've come to appreciate the power of covenant versus contractual relationships, the importance of human attachment, and the critical nature of cognitive distortions that get in the way of our growth as teachers. I've also discovered the value of paying attention in the present, of being "all in." Being present means that you are increasing the likelihood that you will do less harm to yourself and others. I will share both stories and my research on the outcomes of not slowing down and paying attention.

All of this raises another question that applies to ambitious teachers: How can such achievement-driven personalities live more aware lives, lives that aren't beholden to their addiction to achievement?

As a teacher, empathy matters. By trying to understand the reality of others, we demonstrate that someone else matters more than we do. Rollo May said it better when he stated, "Our goal in helping others is to imagine the reality of others."

Authenticity, too, counts for a lot. You can't fool students. If you sit in your office and try to figure out how to do or say something so the students will be impressed or entertained, you have no chance of thriving in the classroom. Through preparation and commitment, you must have something important to say. You should be like a mad scientist who can't wait to get to the classroom to share the experiment. If you adopt this mindset, students will remain intellectually and spiritually in the classroom with you. Students will remember the spirit that you bring to and create in the classroom. Teachers don't have long to convince their audiences that they won't waste their time. Don't give people an excuse to tune you out. By the person you are, the content you provide, and how you transcend the message in word and deed, you can be a great teacher.

Through this journey, you will learn how to create experiences inside others, so they see themselves differently because you have been in their life. I don't believe in entitlement. However, I do believe our students are entitled to have teachers who are their best selves throughout their time together. If there's a single takeaway from this book, it's that becoming your best self not only will make your life better and more successful but will enhance the lives of everyone you teach.

Whether you're a teacher, a student, a business leader, or just someone fascinated by the teaching profession, you'll find this book will instruct, entertain, and—like the best teachers—inspire. When you get right down to it, we're all teachers in one way or another; we teach our students, our employees, our kids, and our friends. So we all have a vested interest in the process. By deconstructing teaching, I hope to dig deep into this process and reveal some truths about how and why we teach the way we do.

ONE

Utah, Wall Street, Harvard

Finding My Place as a Teacher

When someone asked Sir Laurence Olivier what makes a great actor, he responded, "The humility to prepare and the confidence to pull it off." This is the paradox of teaching for me: being humble enough to work hard at designing a potentially great class, and believing in my abilities so that I can turn that potential into reality.

To illuminate this paradox, I'm going to share my journey as a student and observer of teachers. Let's start with some of the first lessons I learned.

On Becoming a Risk-Taking Teacher

I was enthralled with Mr. Walter Stickel and Mr. Ray Snively, my seventh- and eighth-grade teachers at Hosford Elementary School in southeast Portland, Oregon. They always wore nice suits and white shirts, and they smelled as if they had just smoked cigarettes. I loved the smell. I loved how they told stories. When Mr. Snively told a story about the Revolutionary War, I remember holding my breath with excitement. In high school, Mr. Jack Dunn and Miss Roberts could hold my attention for hours (or so it seemed).

I became aware of the huge difference between great and terrible teachers—how I resented the latter and worshipped the former. When I went to college, I had a number of inspirational teachers. I wondered why Stephen Covey could hold my attention in Organizational Behavior 321. I focused as much on his teaching approach—how he told stories, how he paused, how he lowered his voice, how he asked questions in large lecture halls—as I did on his content. It wasn't just what he said, which was great, but how he said it, which was even greater. When Covey spoke, I felt this deep connection with myself. It was as if time stood still. Not to become overly spiritual about it, but it felt like someone was filling my soul with the purest nourishment in existence. As you might imagine, I was thrilled when I became Covey's teaching assistant as a graduate student for the next two years.

I became a close observer of his and other teachers' classroom styles. I was amazed by how teachers differed—how some could anger students by disdainful, disapproving looks while others could bring a classroom to tears by the way they told a story that in lesser teachers might come across as mundane. After my doctoral work at Purdue University and an appointment as a visiting scholar at MIT, I began looking for university teaching jobs. Brigham Young University (BYU) had a compelling draw, given that I knew the school, I had relatives nearby, and my wife wanted to establish her practice in the area as a marriage and family therapist. Most important, I didn't like the other offers I had received from other universities. I ended up signing on to teach in BYU's School of Education rather than their Business School (since the Business School wasn't interested in hiring me). This was the beginning of a pattern—of taking big risks and then hunkering down and making those risks pay off—that would become increasingly apparent over time. Those risks in hindsight don't seem like big leaps. But they were.

Driven to Self-Analysis and Risk

I left my master's degree program early to pursue my doctorate. My wife and I drove a U-Haul truck across the country before I had been accepted into my preferred graduate program. I convinced myself that if I demonstrated my commitment by the long drive without formal acceptance, the admissions committee at Purdue would recognize and reward my resolve. We had no way of making money, no jobs waiting for us, and no friends sitting by the hearth counting the minutes until we arrived. Still, we drove. And I was accepted.

I went to Purdue University because there I could study both organizational behavior and family therapy. I didn't take the typical path to obtain my doctorate—another risk—which resulted in a mixed degree of sorts. When I accepted a postdoc appointment at MIT's Sloan School, I was one of the only postdocs in the program. Once again, I was studying on the margin of a program.

And why did I continue to get more education? Because I operated under the assumption that if I obtained one more degree, I would feel more competent, more settled internally. Yet after achieving each rung on the educational ladder—and later, each rung on the professional one—I felt strangely anxious. I wasn't prepared to get on a professional track, settle in a community, and raise a family. But I never felt like I had a choice—I acted, took risks, and agonized about them reflexively. As we'll explore in more detail in the next chapter, this was my pattern: to act, to risk, and to agonize about it.

BYU's School of Education followed. One friend told me I had sabotaged my own career by joining a university that wasn't considered among the elite. As a newly minted assistant professor, I was self-conscious about working under the aegis of a college with relatively little prestige (compared with the Ivys, for instance). I was defensive. I didn't want to look people in the eye when I told them where I worked.

From my first day on the faculty at BYU, I wondered if I could not only pull off being a professor but carry out all the roles I felt needed to be accomplished simultaneously—a father of two, a good partner, and an active church member. There were also all my worries—about the retirement and care of my parents, about my oldest brother having a near-death experience hang gliding. It all felt like too much. I remember the first morning of my first class that met the day after Labor Day, 1979. I was so anxious that I thought I was having a panic attack. I ran to the restroom and washed my face and breathed deeply, trying to calm myself. Two students asked me if I was OK. I lied and told them I would be fine. Within fifteen minutes, I wandered back into my office, picked up my manila folder, and headed to the classroom, half-hoping no one would show up. I clung to the short-term goal of making it through the day.

What I feared most was running into former professors at the Business School who I was sure were disappointed that I had come back to BYU after attending the school for a master's degree in organizational behavior. I did whatever I could to walk away from their Marriott School of Management. When I did see those former professors—Paul Thompson, Gene Dalton, and Bill Dyer—I was ashamed. There was nothing ever said to me, nor do I know that any of them were embarrassed that I hadn't secured a more prestigious job. But I felt it internally. I would go home and be quiet throughout the evening and ruminate about where I had gone wrong and why I had returned to BYU. My mind was filled with self-critical thoughts.

But the actual work of being a professor suited me. Even though I was a new professor, I realized I could hold students' attention. I could tell good stories. I could learn names easily and use them in the classroom to establish connections with students. At the same time, I also was aware of my flaws as a teacher. I didn't ask good follow-up questions. Connecting abstract ideas in front of the class was difficult for me. My board work was often disorganized.

As you probably have noticed, I was a fierce observer of myself. Outside of class, I noticed that my one-on-one skills counseling students seemed to work. Students usually trusted me immediately. I also observed how my moods changed before teaching and after class was finished. My family was trying to figure out how to deal with these mood swings, not knowing whether I would be exhilarated or depressed based on how class went that day.

I was more obsessed about teaching—about how I affected my students and how they affected me—than were any of my colleagues. I understood very quickly that my obsession had to do with wanting to be the best teacher at the school.

Robert Kegan at the Harvard Graduate School of Education discovered that some individuals remain in what he calls the "interpersonal stage." This stage is defined by activities and actions that are based on how much you please others and define yourself based on how many people you convince of your competence. Life is about accomplishing more tasks than others accomplish. It's about selling others on yourself through your myriad activities. The more tasks you cross off your to-do list, the better person you become.

I related well to this interpersonal stage. It was one of many frameworks that helped me start to make sense of who I was. With hindsight, I became more aware of why I behaved the way I did and taught the way I taught. Let's look back on my journey from West to East, from BYU to Harvard, and my search for a leader who inspired me.

Go East, Young Man

While serving as Brigham Young University's associate dean of Undergraduate Education, I received a call from the associate dean at Harvard

Business School asking me if I would be interested in filling in for a professor to teach the second-year Organizational Behavior course Self-Assessment and Career Development.

I received the call while on a motorcycle trip in southern Utah. We had just pulled into the Bryce Canyon Lodge; my wife and I had taken the trip with my parents, who were almost seventy and riding on my father's Harley. My anxiety level was high—I was concerned about my parents' welfare as they navigated the roads leading to Bryce. When we reached our destination that evening, I was relieved we had made it in one piece. That relief lasted until I called home and received a message to get in touch with Harvard's dean Tom Piper in Boston. When he extended the invitation to teach, I thought immediately that someone was playing a joke on me. When it sank in that it was no joke, I told Tom I would call him back in a few days. From that moment on, my stomach started churning and I couldn't sleep. Should I take this risk? I had never taught using Harvard's case method. I didn't know the material. But people at Harvard had been aware of my research on career theory. I had gained a measure of academic notice through my validating of Edgar Schein's career anchors theory: that each person possesses an anchor consisting of values, motives, and self-perceived talents, and through career experiences refines what is considered important. My research focused on creating a psychometric instrument that identified career anchors.

Harvard was willing to take a chance on me because of what I had accomplished in this area. I figured if they were willing to take a risk on me, I should be willing to take a similar risk on them.

Four months later, after I received permission from BYU to take a leave of absence for a year, our nine-year-old daughter, Sara, and I headed east from Provo, Utah, in our 1977 Buick station wagon pulling a trailer carrying my Harley Davidson. My wife and two other daughters would fly and meet us a bit later in Boston.

From the very beginning, I had doubts. What made me believe I could teach at a school that attracted the best professors in the world?

On January 4, when classes began, I hadn't slept in two days. I had been sick to my stomach throughout most of the holidays.

What will happen if I fail at this? What if I embarrass myself in front of these very smart students? How can I face my colleagues back home if I return a failure? I couldn't shut off the internal noise. When I walked into that first class on a Monday morning, the room was half full; students could shop classes for the first two days. A couple of students got up during my introduction to the course and left the room. Was I losing the class? What had I done to offend? Was I really that boring? What will I do or say if students begin jumping overboard?

I finished the first class. The students filed out. During the fifteen-minute break between this class and my second one, students began trickling into the room. And then a few more. A second-year student introduced himself and asked if he could add the course. Then another. As I began the second class, not only were all the seats taken, but students were sitting in the aisles. No one left the class. More entered. When the class ended, I walked slowly to my office in 435 Baker Library, closed the door, and sobbed with relief.

I knew I could do it. I knew there was hope. Though the self-doubt continues off and on to this day, I realized in that moment thirty years ago that I could stare down fear and win. The process had been agonizing, but I knew the fear could be put back in the bottle.

I sobbed a second time after the year was completed, and we packed up to head back out West. I had survived and thrived in my year of living dangerously. Nothing would ever be the same again.

Returning to the West, I remained there for five more years. But it might have been forever if not for a chance meeting on a plane from Salt Lake City to New York. I was practicing a speech I was scheduled to give when the person sitting next to me asked me to speak up. He introduced himself as John Mack, newly appointed president of Morgan Stanley. One year later, our family moved to New York.

It was a bold decision—leaving a secure academic position for a post in a field and a corporation for which I had little experience or training.

Was I nuts? I didn't know the difference between JP Morgan, Morgan Guarantee, Morgan Stanley, and Stanley Morgan (a receiver for the New England Patriots). I was giving up a deanship, a church community in which I felt valued and accepted, close friends, my family (my father had just passed away and my mother was living nearby), and a reputation as a great teacher. I was leaving the Teaching and Learning Center I had cofounded at BYU, which was involved in the training of faculty and graduate students. I was leaving the prestigious university promotion committee. I was leaving a perfect setting located at the base of the Wasatch Mountains. I was leaving the best motorcycle country in the world. I was leaving access to southern Utah, where my father's roots ran deep.

But I left because I had faith in John Mack, because he felt like a leader. He could teach me about culture and motivation and commitment. So I took a leap of faith to Wall Street with little to no experience in the world of financial services. I realized soon enough that I was just like Dorothy in *The Wizard of Oz* when she looked around at her new surroundings and said, "Toto, I have a feeling we're not in Kansas anymore." I was no longer in the shadows of the Rockies, nestled at the base of Rock Canyon.

I've Come Home

The first day I walked on the trading floor, located at 1221 Avenue of the Americas, I felt like I was home. The characters who occupied this cavernous trading space moved with bravado laced with anxiety. I had never worked with people who were so revved up. David McClelland, in his lengthy and powerful research on motivation, described people who were obsessed with achieving, with accomplishing tasks. At Morgan Stanley, the people were focused myopically on nailing ambitious objectives.

With my academic perspective, Morgan Stanley became a lab to study professionals who had self-selected a work environment in which everyone was a high-need-for-achievement clone. This population informed my interest in and passion for understanding this personality type. Of course, I'd been studying this individual every time I looked in the mirror. *Driven, smart, impatient, successful, autonomous, overscheduled,* and *committed* were words that described me, too. From intensely personal experience, I knew this type couldn't achieve all the agenda items on his list of responsibilities and action items. I knew that when this personality type felt overwhelmed, guilt (over things left undone) was an emotional reflex. This individual always came up short, no matter how much he tried. There was never enough time. Ever.

And having arrived at Morgan Stanley and witnessing employees all around me striving to achieve stretch goals and outdo the other person, I saw I was with kindred spirits. Home sweet home. Or so I thought until I realized what I had gotten myself into.

Failing to Fit

Why do I continue to place myself in situations that test my mettle? Because I relish challenges—even challenges that are difficult or impossible to meet. Morgan Stanley tested me every day. Could I have ten tough conversations daily during a rough week? Could I fire dozens of people? Could I manage hundreds of talent management experts around the world 24/7? Could I be a compass of sorts for John Mack, one of the most dynamic, intriguing, gifted motivators I'd ever met? Could I push back with him and other senior professionals who saw me as a competent social scientist but not "one of the boys"? Could I nurture and support my wife and kids as they suffered through the transition to a new place and a very different environment?

I thought I'd be better at being a manager than I was. I assumed I would learn over time not to take slights to heart and would be able to brush them off. But I couldn't. John would say, "Just look at it as a game. You can't take this stuff so personally." But I did.

Observing John, I realized that the best leaders also possess qualities that make great teachers. John worked with me; he listened to me the way top teachers engage with their students. I don't think I've ever met anyone who listened as well as John Mack did. I felt completely understood. There were moments he would be frustrated with me. There were times I wasn't sure I could trust him. But just as I had faith in him, he had faith in me.

Like the best teachers, John was able to compartmentalize and focus on the task at hand. Unlike some leaders, he didn't just talk at you. Instead, he concentrated intently, asking good questions and making comments appropriate to your concerns. He made you feel like the most important person in the company, the same way some teachers make each student feel like he or she is the most important one in the classroom.

As a teacher, I always want to make students feel psychologically safe. John has the same effect on his people, and they were encouraged to take reasonable risks without fear of making mistakes.

In fact, John modeled this behavior and took a chance with me. I had made my preference known early on: an office next to John so that I would have some referent power, given that I wasn't a banker. Soon I had a target on my back. Other senior leaders were jealous of John and my relationship. Most were intimidated by John, and they didn't like that this new naïve guy, an outsider no less, had John's ear.

I felt I was disappointing a boss I revered and sometimes feared. It seemed as if I had swung for the fences and come up short. When John and Phil Purcell, former CEO of Dean Witter, announced that the two entities were merging, I knew I had to leave. I didn't believe in the merger. I didn't believe in my own abilities. I didn't believe in Phil

Purcell. I couldn't understand how John could believe in him. How had he and I lost our moorings in such different ways?

Being Open to the Mysteries of Chance

Earlier that year, Kim Clark, dean of Harvard Business School, had been visiting Morgan Stanley offices to meet with our chairman, Richard Fisher, who was a noted alum of Harvard Business School. Kim had been a friend of mine through our church affiliation. We ran into one another in the hallway on the thirty-ninth floor of 1585 Broadway, headquarters of Morgan Stanley. We spoke for two minutes. He asked me to give him a call in the next few days. From the minute he asked me to call, I couldn't think of anything else. I lay awake at night wondering what he wanted to talk about. I fantasized that Kim would be my way out. I found myself breaking my cardinal rule of never running from or to something. I was imagining doing both.

When I called Kim two days later, I flashed back to the moment I phoned Sally Iverson, the first girl I fell for as a freshman in high school. I had dry mouth. I was sweating through my shirt. I knew Kim. I trusted him. Why was I regressing back to old feelings of not measuring up? Of being rejected? When Kim and I connected, he mentioned that the Business School was experimenting with bringing practitioners in to help connect the faculty with the real world. We would be expected to teach a full load, write cases, and bring intellectual capital to the game. He asked me if I would be interested. I would need to interview with members of the Organizational Behavior (OB) Department; they would determine if they wanted me to join their group for a trial run.

I spent a day in Boston interviewing. From the lack of universal enthusiasm during the interviews, I could sense that not everyone was keen on the idea of bringing me in as a practitioner professor. As I was heading off campus to grab a taxi and go back to New York,

I bumped into Len Schlesinger, an old friend and head of the service management area. When he heard why I was on campus and I explained my OB Department interviews, he asked if I would be interested in teaching in his group. I knew little about the field of service management, but didn't dismiss his suggestion out of hand. A few days later, I heard from the OB group that they didn't see a fit. They had a number of faculty who were researching careers, and there was too much overlap with other faculty. The next day, Len called to see if I'd come up to Boston and interview with his group. I did. And we clicked.

Kim Clark and Len Schlesinger were two excellent leaders, and I observed them in action. They both had clear goals and enthusiasm for the school—the faculty and students. Len Schlesinger would try anything, believing anything was possible. I was amazed, and continue to be amazed, at his lack of self-doubt. Kim was dean for eighteen months, and he told me that he was having a great time being dean. He could have been speaking Chinese. I couldn't fathom how anyone could thrive and love having so much responsibility. Len felt like he could be the president of the university and do it comfortably. I was in awe. I was also experiencing those old feelings of inadequacy during this transition. Why was I so filled with self-doubt? Five months later I joined the faculty, commuting from New York.

Office Assignments and the Case Method

The cards and letters and phone calls kept pouring in from friends and family far and near, expressing excitement about my appointment to the faculty of Harvard Business School. During the winter, I had been sitting in on classes in Boston. I watched Jim Cash, Gary Loveman, Linda Hill, Jeffrey Rayport, Len Schlesinger, Jim Heskett. After every class, I noted what I learned from each teacher. And with every learning came more fear and self-doubt. Each teacher possessed a strength that eluded me. Loveman had command of the class; he didn't even need notes to teach—he was so strong he could just rely on his brain. Len brought enthusiasm and support and positive confrontation. Rayport pulled concepts out of thin air and synthesized the student responses magically. I watched and perseverated. And I wouldn't teach until the fall, five months away. I had plenty of time to nurture my fear. But I realized that observing others was a key strategy in figuring out our own teaching style. While sitting in on others' classes took time, and at times made me uncomfortable, I knew that this comparative processing of how the case method was done by others would give me more courage to try other approaches.

Let me describe Harvard's case method here and explain how it affected my teaching. As its name implies, the case method involves teaching through stories and narratives. Typically, instructors use the Socratic Method to help students think about the managerial challenges the cases present and respond to them. The Socratic Method consists of the teacher asking a question to a student, having the student reply, followed by a subsequent question. The design of the teaching plan basically follows this question and response sequence. The method consists of asking questions to students, followed by a response from the students, followed by another question from the professor. Guided by teachers, students create solutions to case-related problems. At other universities as well as in high schools and other educational settings, teachers use variations on the case method (though they may not refer to it as the case method). Stories are a universal method to convey knowledge.

The case method has had an effect on my class preparation. My pre-class focus on tone of voice, for instance, became crucial to my teaching, because the case method relies on stories and metaphor to pull the students into problem situations that need to be solved. As for any good storyteller, how you begin your story is critical.

I learned that at Harvard Business School, we would tell our stories in front of a semicircle of eighty students—it's referred to as "teaching in the pit"—and facilitate discussions about the case. The first part of a class is typically about "sense making." What's the case about, what's the analysis, who are the players? The second part of the class is about "choice making." Given the information we've discussed, what should we do? What are the actions or nonactions that would make sense for this situation? The discussion throughout the eighty-minute time period is a give and take between the teacher and students, and between the students and each other.

It took me a while to develop this particular approach to case method teaching, but watching other faculty members use it was instructive, as was my proximity to so many masters of the method.

David Garvin, a gifted professor at the Business School, had the ability to organize his thinking in a way that was precise, clear, and straightforward. His blackboards were well thought out, and he had perfect handwriting. David spoke slowly and enunciated every word. He was in no hurry. He mesmerized me with the way he constructed his sentences and his clear, methodological approach to his teaching style. Observing him was frightening because of his ability, but it soon became exhilarating. At first, I reminded myself that "I will never be able to do what he does." Yet his love for teaching was apparent, and it relaxed me so that I could pay attention to every nuance of his teaching.

When I walked to my new office, I noted that one adjacent office belonged to an internationally known Organizational Behavior faculty member. Michael Tushman was recognized for his innovative approaches to research in organizations. He wrote books and journal articles. And he wrote a lot. Later, when I visited his home, I couldn't help but notice that his house was perfectly decorated. The perfect residence for the perfect professor. Of course, I hadn't written in the field for years. No books, no articles, no cases. What was I doing next to Mike? Seeing his office unoccupied during my first few days there, I asked his assistant if he was traveling that week. I was informed that he was at his summer home. One more reason to hate him. How would I be able to walk by his office and not feel inferior, not compare, not get overwhelmed with the road ahead?

The good news? The occupant of the office on the other side made me forget about my jealousy of Michael. Bob Merton won the Nobel Prize at age forty-six, having discovered with his colleagues the financial trading model called Black-Scholes. Bob dressed very well, cared about appearance, drove a Jaguar, and loved playing poker. He was naturally quiet, funny, and gracious. Most important to me, he was brilliant.

Sandwiched between Mike and Bob, I couldn't get to my office without being reminded that I had come up short in my life and career. Bob was writing papers I could barely decipher. He had noted scientists and scholars visiting daily. I spent my time making sure my pencils were sharpened and that I had plenty of my favorite pens in both black and dark blue ink. I fluctuated between hiding in my office after duct-taping the door shut when I knew Mike and Bob were in the office and leaving it wide open so that someone would stop by and welcome me to the fold. It was a bimodal approach. Bob, Mike, and I were all the same age. Both of them were teaching in executive education courses, while I would focus on a second-year elective course centered on understanding leadership in the context of professional service firms. I knew they would have large audiences.

From my earlier experience teaching at the school, I was aware that I would need to earn a reputation and generate student interest through my own devices. I had no reputation as a teacher. I would be competing with Michael Porter, Rosabeth Moss Kanter, and Clay Christensen. More importantly, I would be competing with my own internal narrative of self-doubt, my belief I may not succeed.

It struck me that the first class would make or break me. The students could come and go during class and assess whether or not they wanted to spend a semester with me as the teacher. Would I be able to remember Laurence Olivier and how he defined great acting? Would his definition empower or cripple me? How would I be able to summon my best self to show up for the first day of class?

No doubt, most teachers in new and challenging situations pose these types of anxious questions to themselves. What I was to learn is that these questions reflect particular patterns—patterns that may provide insights for teachers and leaders.

TWO

First Class

Anxious Thoughts, Preparations, and Patterns

What will I do before the session begins that illustrates that I value the content more than anything? If I believe I should be like a mad scientist inviting the students into the laboratory, what has to happen before the lab is opened to students? If I am to convince students that they mean more to me than anyone else, what must happen before I ever set foot in the classroom setting?

I've read the case at least five times in preparation, and more if it's the first time I'm teaching the case. I've read it considering the student questions that have been posed. I've read it with yellow marker in hand. I've read it looking for content that might be confusing to me. I've read it reflecting on what the students have learned or what I wanted them to learn from the previous class period.

I need to know the story better than anyone else, so that I have the flexibility to zig and zag—to move from point to point in sometimes un-expected but hopefully enlightening ways. In the beginning of my teaching career, I was more didactic, wanting to move logically and quickly from Point A to Point B. Now I like the surprise of connecting the unlikely dots of Points D and X.

Where does the case fit into the overall module or course? It is essential to get the sequencing of why you are teaching this case at this present time. To enhance the learning, the cases must have a particular flow to them. Thus, the case has to provide a taste of the challenges and theories that will be introduced through the subsequent cases in the module. If the topic is teams, then our case discussion must push students to question the effectiveness of individual efforts versus working in teams with appropriate performance metrics.

If I begin the module with this case, I need to ensure that at some point (typically at the end of the session) I articulate and make explicit how this case is an introduction to the various issues that we'll study during the module. The sequencing of the cases presupposes that I've created a plan for the day that builds on the previous day's theory so that students understand how the content is grounded on different levels of theory. If the theory doesn't hold together sequentially, the students may become confused about the intent and purpose of the session. Understanding the rhyme and reason of the particular class session reduces the mood swing by sabotaging my either/or thinking.

What might the students be thinking or feeling when reading the case? In the case of C&S Grocers, for example, a number of students not only won't know the business of wholesale grocers but won't have particular interest in the topic. It will be seen as "old world" like studying a manufacturing plant in Cleveland, Ohio. The students might question why we would assign a case that doesn't focus on something sexy and relevant—startups, for instance. I have to have faith that the story or the tension in the story will make them curious. In the C&S case, I introduce early that a father has asked his twenty-eight-year-old son to take over the nearly one-hundred-year-old family business. The father has asked the protagonist's two older brothers to run the business, but they don't want anything to do with it. The protagonist is roughly the same age as the students; this commonality may prompt students to ask the questions, "Could I run a business at twenty-eight? Could I deal with the pressures of running a family business? And the business isn't even a viable company when the central figure is asked to run the business." I've tried to create enough intrigue in the early pages so that the students focus less on the industry and more on the problem at hand. In posing a dilemma or tension point early, I'm enticing the reader to read on.

Method behind the Madness: Contingencies at Every Turn

Does the teaching plan I've created have any rhyme or reason? Should I follow the typical teaching plan in which case facts are generated from the case so that we can make sense of what might flow into an action plan? And as usual, the students have other things on their minds; they are obsessing about their own identities within the school, the section, with roommates, with old acquaintances, with new friends—they may be ending relationships they held dear, and more.

My intent is to teach the students how to "crack" a case. I want to teach them a methodology of studying that is consistent with what they are learning in their other classes. Thus, while I may feel certain constraints regarding the teaching plan, I am also optimistic because at the start of the semester, students are more malleable, more tentative, more concerned with their images. Using a relatively formal case study approach allows me to be more aware of the students' reactions—their excitement, their abject fear, their worry over embarrassing themselves in front of eighty-nine new "friends."

When I take the time to reflect, I'm struck by how overwhelming it can be to manage the multiple, interactive levels of activities, situations, and processes inherent in teaching: the beginning of the semester and how it impacts the nature of the case-teaching plan; my particular approach to the plan; how I relate with the ninety students in order to teach them class norms, processes on how to study cases, and how to respond to one another in class; and communicating the case content.

New teachers tend to focus on the content more than anything else because they are confident in their grasp of the subject matter. On some unconscious level, they obsess about proving to the students that they "know their stuff." Too often, they go one step further by trying to prove they are the smartest individual in the room. That is seldom the case at any graduate school, including Harvard—because when it's one against thirty or one hundred or more, the group wins. The deck is stacked in favor of the students. Their collective experiences, IQs, and confidence will beat the instructor every time. And if the deck is stacked in favor of the students, there is some probability that self-doubt may creep into play.

So I try to focus on interrelationships between various teaching elements rather than proving myself superior to the students. For instance: Does my teaching plan connect with the study questions? Each case the students prepare will have two or three study questions to assist them in framing their study of the case. However, I need to train students on the multidimensional aspects of the puzzle they are trying to figure out. And using the same questions posed earlier as guides in the teaching plan emphasizes regurgitating facts rather than seeing different aspects of the organization. If, for example, I'm teaching the Rob Parson case and the study questions focus on whether or not the protagonist should be promoted, or what the nature of the performance management system is, I might consider beginning the in-class conversation focused on the nature of the work in financial services, or homing in on why Morgan Stanley has entered the business of debt capital markets. But to simply ask students to answer the study questions during the case conversation actually creates inertia, dissipating the energy and excitement in the conversation.

The goal is to see the elephant from different vantage points. Separating the study questions from the plan ensures that a richer conversation will ensue. The curriculum, if it works, will answer the study questions, but in a less direct way.

I need to understand: Have I thought through whether I'm going to do most of the talking or if I want the students to be engaged in the conversation? How will I divide up the eighty minutes so there are different approaches being used? Have I identified the students I want to participate given their background, content expertise, or geographical reach and experience? What student is struggling to keep up or has a crisis in his life? How will I draw him in? Will my boards tell a story? Why will I be using them? What's the rationale behind their use? Will I use them for a review at the end of the course?

Knowing the Students

It seems so simple. What teacher wouldn't make the effort to familiarize himself with his students before class begins, or to establish the classroom ground rules? And yet, so many other things occupy the mind of a teacher that, unfortunately, this simple task often goes unattended. Therefore, I remind myself to pay attention to this task. However, if I've studied the students and they know I know their backgrounds, I am more likely to avert disaster.

A litany of questions and self-instructions run through my head before this first class. Here is a sampling of the thoughts flowing through my mind:

Learn about your students. Ask for class cards before you begin the teaching process. Learn how to pronounce their names. Know whether or not they have had previous, relevant experiences. Call them by name the first day of class. Ideally, use table tents (name cards) so you can quickly attach a name to a face. Table tents allow the teacher and other students to know one anothers' names. Some teachers go the whole semester without ever using their students' names. In the syllabus, note how students can contact you. Set the expectation the first day of class that you expect to be used as a resource for content conversations as well as career advice.

Do any of your students have learning disabilities? Is there anything that might detract from the learning experience? Perhaps a student is visually impaired and struggles to see the board. Do you already know any of the students? Do you already have favorites? Is there a student with whom you've had a negative interaction? Should you speak to the person beforehand? Ask yourself what the students will be nervous about on the first day. How much content should you share, or will the first class be primarily administrative, setting expectations?

How many women are represented in the class? What about international students? Married or single? Socioeconomic diversity is important to me, and I know I'm likely to make judgments based on limited amounts of information—their home towns, schools attended, clothes, and accessories.

I will be dividing them into groups of six for intensive interaction after the class has concluded. They will meet for two hours after class to discuss the class session and go over specific assignments in the smaller groups. How will I divide them? I will need to have diversity around gender, age, previous work experience, college experience, and whether the students were in the same sections in their first year. I want to avoid grouping close friends together; I want them to meet new and different people.

As I prepare for the first class, I sit back and ask myself if my students could choose any teacher to teach Organizational Behavior or Authentic Leadership, would they prefer someone else to me? More important, would I want to be taught by me? How will the students experience themselves because they have had an interaction with me in the classroom?

Preparing for the First Day of Class . . . and My Anxieties

Well before the first class period of the semester, I visit the classroom where I'll be teaching. I walk to the four corners of the room, sit down in different seats, and reflect. Rob Kaplan, head of the Federal Bank of Dallas, used to go to his assigned class days before it began and stand in front of an empty room and simulate a class. At times he would bring a few colleagues with him, and we'd sit around the room and be cold-called. Rob never acted self-conscious or worried what we might think. We role-played as if it were a full classroom of first-year students. Rob wanted to hear his own voice in the class. He needed to hear himself asking certain questions to see if they sounded right or forced or off point. When I heard Rob talk about this exercise, I found myself admiring his brave idea and surprised at how "out of my comfort zone" it made me feel—Rob was allowing himself to be vulnerable in a way that was scary.

After visiting the classroom, I reflect on what I'm going to say in class and how it may affect different students. Will my approach ensure that different learning styles are respected and valued? For students who are more visceral, will I use enough metaphors that help them internalize what I hope they draw from the session through story? Will I use a role play to illustrate how difficult it is to terminate someone so that the students can viscerally feel, see, and experience peripherally what it would be like? For students who depend on the sense of vision to take in knowledge, will I use the boards to guide their cognitive journey? When I'm telling a story to make a point, how will I use tone and how will I raise and lower my voice to underscore a point? When will I whisper to draw students closer?

I deal with these preclass anxieties by arriving early, setting up the room and my notes, walking up to students and asking them how they are doing, or acknowledging students when they enter the room by name. This is all self-serving because it reduces the ratio of ninety to one, allowing me to relate to individuals rather than to the large group. It makes the students more human, more approachable, more fallible, and more vulnerable in a positive way. It changes the nature of the communication pattern from a vertical (where I'm talking down to them with the answers) to a more horizontal relationship. It means that I treat them more like adults, full and equal partners in the learning process, rather than acting like I'm the source of all knowledge. If I create an atmosphere in which they expect me to deliver all the answers, they will settle back in their seats and wait for the answers rather than actively participate. Because I expect the students to assume some responsibility for the classroom learning, I want to connect before class with a few students to create an inclusive start to the process and reduce my anxiety of facing the multitudes alone.

Take My Words with a Grain of Salt

As I reflect on what I've written so far, I realize the implication is that I'm prescribing my approach to all teachers. Yet there are teachers who arrive in class with no notes and can masterfully involve and include students in the learning process. They can be hypnotic in their ability to transform the learning experience into a memorable classroom adventure. I don't have that ability. I do have anxiety, and so I'm sharing my ways of coping with it.

I tell myself the night before I teach students: I know I'm effective and that I'm prepared and have a good sense of self as a teacher. Nonetheless, I'm still filled with self-doubt. I can meditate or jog or watch trash TV, but to no avail. The morning I teach, I know that I won't want to eat or to talk to anyone. I know that I'll declare to Dakota, the faculty specialist, that I never want to teach again. I know it will happen even after thirty-five years of teaching. I will seriously think about retiring or changing professions hours before I enter the classroom. So rather than perseverating in my office, I must move physically. I must get up and head to the teaching room early. Rather than listen to irrational thoughts and feelings, I need to engage with the "enemy." I need to look students in the eyes and engage. I need to get out of my head and be interested in something other than my thoughts and feelings and insecurities.

The pattern that surfaces is the either/or syndrome. Will I leave the classroom with a feeling of either success or failure?

So even if you aren't a teacher who is wrapped up in your own doubts and insecurities, you should know what your patterns are—the tendencies and habits that either serve or disrupt your effectiveness. I urge you to teach your way. But I would also urge you to consider what your style is. How do you put yourself in a position to put your best teaching foot forward in order to bless the lives of your students?

I have to ask this question of myself regularly. Recently, I forgot to do so. My latest batch of students experienced me as a bit distracted when I entered the classroom and as I began class. They believed that I was fitting class between other activities that were more important to me. I didn't stay true to my basic principle of preparing and calming myself and being present in every way.

Arriving at the Classroom

What are the implications when, as a teacher, you arrive one minute before the class is to begin? What do you communicate? Do students care about when you arrive? What you are wearing? Notice the cleanliness of the classroom—for example, whether the boards have been erased. Is the temperature of the classroom too hot or too cold? Are there enough chairs? Is there chalk? Is the audiovisual system running properly? What is different about the room that the students might recognize and that might become a distraction? Is the previous teacher in the classroom speaking with students from her class? Is the clock set to the right time?

To become aware of these factors when you arrive late might mean that they become a problem while you are teaching. If you show up a minute before the class begins, is there a chance you may begin the class late? If you sense you are in a hurry, what does that signal to your students? If you don't make eye contact with your students because you are focusing on teaching notes, what does that signal? Every activity, from when you enter the classroom to whether or not you end on time, communicates multiple messages. As the instructor, you need to increase the probability that your students will see and experience and feel what you want them to experience. If you are running late or are in a rush, students could very well believe that you're not fully invested in teaching them. They may not give you the benefit of the doubt if they believe that you're fitting them in between other tasks that seem more important to you.

Remember, it doesn't matter what your intentions are as a teacher. Intentionality only goes so far. The key is what the students experience in the classroom. How do they experience themselves when they see you leading the class or conversing with them one-to-one? You do not get to vote on how they interpret your efforts as a teacher either in front of the class or in your office. If a student comes up to you in the minute before class begins and asks a question and you never make eye contact, the student and those observing the interaction will interpret what they see and hear. They won't know what you are thinking or feeling. You may have intended to be interested, empathic, and helpful, but their interpretation will be far from your intent.

How students react to you has a lot to do with when you arrive in the classroom and how you prepare to begin the class. I try to get to the classroom as early as possible. Twenty minutes beforehand isn't too early. I want to visit every corner of the room every time I teach to get a feel for the environment. I mentioned earlier checking media support, boards, temperature, chalk, students, and more. I want to come early to deal with my nerves. If I picture facing ninety smart, driven, and time-sensitive students the night before, I can easily imagine myself as Daniel in the lions' den.

Fifteen Minutes before Takeoff

When I enter the room, I consider what I should write on the board. I also walk to the back of the room to grasp the view from the "cheap seats." I go through my list of to-dos as the time ticks down. Practice speaking in the room as you would the first day of class, I tell myself. Give a mini lecture. Or, if you can convince colleagues to join you, have two or three sit in various seats around the room and listen to you practice. You don't have to wait for fifteen minutes before class starts. You can rehearse at any time, donning your teaching attire so the first day of class doesn't feel too foreign. I'm suggesting that you role-play yourself. Understand that you own that space. It is sacred for the eighty minutes that you share it with students. Bring your attitude and spirit and intentions into the room well before you teach your first class. The class should feel like an old friend whom you look forward to visiting, not a foreign, uncomfortable space akin to a new city in a different country.

Here is what I promise will happen. As many times as you visit the room and become comfortable with your surroundings, something will occur on the first day that will be unexpected. A student will want an answer to a question that throws you off. He will want to know if he can bring his dog to class and whether he has to ask permission from the registrar. Someone will be pregnant and will want to sit next to one of the exits so she can leave the room quickly—and these exit-area seats will have already been taken. Someone will have poor eyesight and request that you write extra-large on the board. Three students will want to add the class at the last moment "because it's the most important class in our graduate program." One of them wants to take it from home. Could you arrange that the course be video recorded for him? And minutes before class begins, you realize you dropped part of your peanut butter and jam sandwich on your pants, leaving a stain of both the butter and the jam. Because this is the first time you've taught in the building, you have no idea where the restroom is. And class begins in seven minutes.

Finally, a colleague walks by your room, sees you, and asks if you can go to dinner in two weeks at his house with two other couples. As your colleague leaves, you look up and see a light in the ceiling that is flickering off and on. Is there time to replace it? Are you the only one who will notice it? It feels like the biggest distraction possible at the worst possible time. As the clock ticks down to the starting time, you notice a student wiping her eyes as if she has been crying. Or is it allergies? Or have you done something unintended that has made her weep? As you begin the class, you suddenly panic and realize you haven't turned off your cell phone. Or have you?

Beginning the First Class

The first five minutes of the course are the most important of the day and of the semester. How you begin will set expectations. The tone, the use of the boards, and the spatial distance between you and the students communicate your intentions. How loud you speak matters. It all matters. It matters because the students have expectations about what the experience is going to be like. From what they've heard and read about you—or if they've taken courses from you previously—they have expectations of how you facilitate, govern, and teach the class.

Beginning on time communicates that you care about their time, about their lives, how they learn, and the importance of learning. When you begin on time, you communicate your intention to keep the time sacred. You are telling students that every moment in class is priceless, never to return. You are demonstrating how sacred you hold them as participants in the learning experience. You are reinforcing how sacred you hold the content of the course, what is to be learned, and how it is to be learned. Most important, you are communicating that you hold them in high esteem. You are saying to them that they are adults; that they deserve all your energy for the next eighty minutes; that you aren't looking down on them from a perch of all knowingness, but that you are full and equal partners in this endeavor.

Some teachers begin class with administrative information. Others start with various types of information that don't capture the interest or hearts of the students. These small start-time decisions are big decisions.

I like to begin each class with a story that represents an objective of the course or subtext of the course. By telling a compelling story or parable, I hope to capture the students' hearts, their attention. I want to pull them into the experience by painting a picture to which they can relate. When I teach a case like C&S Grocers, a story about the dramatic growth of a wholesale grocer, I tell them of a twenty-eight-year-old son of the owner, who is asked by his father to take over the business. An example:

> *You are working on the docks as a twenty-eight-year-old in Worcester, Massachusetts, and your father asks you to stop work for a moment so he can talk with you. He tells you that the business isn't doing well, that your older brothers don't want to work in the business, and that he wants you to take over—not in a year, but next week. He wants you to deal with the unions and the aftermath of a flood that cost millions of dollars of inventory. He wants you to consider moving the business to Vermont. Your father begins to cry, telling you*

that he feels like a failure. He feels like he has ruined the business his father began in the early 1900s. And he wants you to save the business.

Through the story of Rick Cohen, I have invited the students to join me emotionally and psychologically in this adventure called Organizational Behavior. I have invited them to become cotravelers with me on this journey for the next eighty minutes. I have invited them into my "mad scientist lab." And I need their focus and interest to be inside the classroom, with me and with the other travelers.

Seeking Common Ground

That focus and interest, however, depend to some extent on factors that have nothing to do with me or the class. You see, I don't know what has been happening in the lives of the students. However, I do know that some probably would have been out drinking the night before class. Or a few of them might have broken up with their girlfriend or boyfriend. A few will show up to class not feeling particularly well, with colds, or fevers, or lacking sleep. Others will have parents or siblings who are ailing or going through difficult transitions in their lives. Some students will have taken a test the day before in another class with the knowledge that the test didn't go well. And some will be dealing with the conflict between traveling home to see their families and attending a campus party on the coming weekend. Other students may not have prepared for class as well as they should have; they studied for someone else's course and not yours. And of course, some will be hungry, and some will be yearning for a cup of coffee.

By beginning with a story, I'm trying to provide students with a similar framework for learning the concepts of the day. Through storytelling, I hope to create a common experience that engages all their senses.

I don't have the luxury to begin the class in a leisurely manner—time is too precious. I want students on the edge of their seats from the moment they sit. I have invited them into the lab. I don't request it. I use metaphor as a means to create the collective experience.

If I have announcements to make, I insert them after a story so that students are listening. They know the setting and the case for discussion, and they will be listening more intently to announcements about when papers might be due, when the next exam will be administered, and so on. However, much of the administrative content can be communicated through other processes, whether it be through a website or a course syllabus. Determining when to make announcements may seem like small stuff, but it's actually a big decision. If you make them too early, you may lose student intensity, interest, and focus. If you decide to hold off on announcements too long, the students may be focusing on festering questions: Do I have to hand in a hard copy of the paper? Can I have extra time?

Take a Cue from Other Teachers

You possess a distinct style of teaching, and you want to stick to that style—that's what will convey your authenticity to a class. At the same time, make it a habit to think about other teachers' styles. It can help you make adjustments that will make you a more effective teacher, especially as it relates to your storytelling. Observe other teachers in the school. Beware during the process of watching other teachers that you aren't comparing as much as reflecting on your style. Know that "trying on different styles" is part of the evolution of your teaching style.

Do you know why you speak the way you do? Jim Austin, a former professor at Harvard Business School (HBS), used to begin his classes speaking very quietly. He wanted the students to lean forward and feel as if they were hearing something very special. He might start out in a voice barely above a whisper, "Today, you are going to go inside a re-markable company that you've never heard of. And you will never forget it once you visit it." This approach puts students on notice that they are going to have a unique experience; that only those sixty students in the classroom will have this experience. It also communicates that the students will need to be paying attention and keeps them on the edge of their seats.

While I prefer beginning with a story and Jim Austin uses a dramatic whisper, other professors are just as strategic in their beginning class moments. Jan Rivkin of the Strategy department at HBS opens with a puzzle. For example, he asks: Coors versus Anheuser Busch? One of these companies is growing with double-digit growth; the other is in gradual decline. They've both been making beer the same amount of time. What differentiates them? Which one would you invest in?

David Garvin, former professor who passed away in 2018, began by offering students choices. He might describe a story's protagonist very briefly and then say, "Today, we need to figure out whether our protagonist is brilliant, naïve, or just lucky."

So we have a story, a whisper, a puzzle, and a choice, all valid alternatives to begin a class. Each instructor leans or depends on a particular approach. I use story, knowing that it will take two to three minutes to set the stage. But I believe it's worth using that time, given that I'm trying to pull the students into a common consciousness and attempting to do so by inviting them into a scene viscerally. Have I tried the other approaches? All but the whisper. Do I believe in the other approaches? Yes! But each instructor should experiment, trying at least one other approach (see Ibarra, "The Authenticity Paradox"). Through observing other approaches and through my own experimentation, I realized that storytelling also pulls me into this common consciousness, and so I'm having a similar experience with the students. We are all in this together. While there are times when I use other methods, storytelling is often my starting point.

Early on, students begin to expect a story or parable. I often reflect back on reading stories to my daughters when tucking them into bed. These students are being invited into a similarly altered state of relaxation but also a learning state. I am like a hypnotist swinging an old-fashioned timepiece in front of the patient. With the cue of the story, the students begin to surrender to the spirit of the class. Students of Austin, Rivkin, and Garvin also begin their psychological journey based on the cues given by their respective professors.

I've spent a significant amount of space writing about the first five minutes of class. Why am I going into so much detail? Because I don't want the new teacher to spend all eighty minutes parrying with students or using unnecessary energy and effort to keep them engaged, or worse, trying to convince them of their superior knowledge from the outset of the class and never winning them over.

There is no more difficult task than trying to "win over" students. You will find yourself working harder and harder trying to create a space in which the class carries the conversation. Unless you reach some modicum of flow, the classroom will feel more like a boxing ring than a place for learning and vulnerability and courageous conversations. You will find yourself in a defensive mode right from the start. Your view of students will shift and you'll perceive them more as opponents than partners in the learning adventure. Win them over now. Don't wait until the thirtieth minute or the fiftieth minute. Create the context in which the probability increases that students will be working with you as opposed to against you.

Irrational Imaginations: Preparing for Class

Your particular environment—the philosophy of a particular school, the content of a particular course—determines how you prepare for your class. At Harvard, much of my preclass thought and anxiety is about a class I teach called Authentic Leadership. It's a class that asks a lot from the students emotionally, and it can turn into an emotional roller coaster. Perhaps that is why I find myself writing more about anxiety and fear than most faculty might. But the questions I pose to students require transparency and disclosure, both from the students and from myself. Modeling behavior is central to the outcome I want to achieve. The key component of my teaching model is to be the example of authenticity.

My class preparation varies by seasons. If it's winter, the students may feel they have figured out how to get by in school. Thus, I need to prepare for a certain degree of complacency. In the fall, there is more energy and excitement around this new adventure of beginning an MBA. In this instance, I try to capitalize on this inherent interest and involvement. I also prefer teaching in the fall, in part because I like how the students arrive with a fresh perspective on this new experience. The time of day, too, is critical for me and perhaps less so for students (some sign up for courses based on what fits their schedule rather than their interest in a topic).

I find myself freshest in the morning and would like to teach the first class at 8:30 a.m. Yet family considerations alter this preference, since I take some responsibility for launching my kids into their daily activities. The second class period begins at 10:05 a.m. It's the most popular time to teach for faculty because the students are fresher and have mainly recovered from the previous night's activities. The students also like this time period because their coffee and roll will carry them through until lunch time. The third session runs through lunch. The students begin to get antsy and distracted in the waning minutes of the class period. Hunger takes over. As Abraham Maslow and his hierarchy of needs demonstrate, basic requirements like the need to eat can sabotage my efforts to hold student interest.

For eighteen years here in Boston, I have wanted to teach in the first part of the week and not the end of the week. I wanted to finish by Wednesday and gloat over my colleagues who would be working while I was off. Two years ago, I taught at the end of the week and realized how much nicer I was to my family the weekend before I taught. Later, I'll go into excruciating (for me and my family) detail about how I made everybody around me miserable as I prepared psychologically for the beginning of class. Once I experimented with teaching at the tail end of the week, I noticed how pleasant my life became during weekends.

I assign seats. I know no one wants to sit close to the professor. Most of them think, "The farther away from Professor DeLong, the better." I want students to sit next to students they don't know well, so that when we have dyadic conversations between students, personal discoveries emerge based on a lack of familiarity with their nearby classmates.

I also know that a few students aren't sure they want to take the course. They have heard that they should take it—perhaps their friends have recommended it to them as a way to foster interpersonal aware-ness. But even the students who were sure they wanted to take the course may be nervous because they know the class won't simply be straight case method teaching. It will consist of myriad experiences that will push them to be more reflective about how they impact others because of their behavior.

Given all this, my presence during that first class can have either a positive or a negative influence on students' perceptions. How do I man-age the impact I have on my students? By being reflective and self-analytical. And the way I do this is by asking myself a series of questions about who I'm teaching for:

- Are my needs being sequenced before those of my students?

- Is there anything I care deeply about that I want to communi-cate to students about me?

- By dressing up conservatively and looking stern, am I going to convince students that this is a hard course?

- Am I going to convince them that I'm a tough guy, a disciplinar-ian, someone to take seriously?

- What will I do to convince students that I'm smart, that I could have taught a finance course (though that's a stretch)?

- If students have been told by friends that the course is easy, how might I change their minds?

Notice that the questions I've posed are about me and impression management. The questions are about drama and manipulation and coercion.

What happened to those pure motives about helping students live more fulfilling lives? What happened to that person who spent six months redesigning the course in order to give students a more meaningful class? If it's all about me, the students will sense it almost immediately. For this reason, first impressions count. It's why the first class is the most important class of the semester. It is the one that sets the standard for openness, for congruence, for being vulnerable. To achieve this ideal objective, I must focus on the moment at hand and create the kind of experience I would want from a great teacher. I believe this moment between teacher and student can change both of us for good, and it's the type of change that begins with that first class.

Finally, as much as I don't want to admit it, the fear does lie below the surface that I won't succeed. Conversely, flying without a net is incredibly exciting. As class begins, I'm filled with self-doubt and either/or thinking—either perfection or failure. I try to get past these doubts and either/ors. If I can get past them, I can attend to the moment. I will be aware and ready to make the class a great one, and not just routine.

Emerging Patterns

As you read about my thoughts and behaviors before and during class, you may have thought to yourself, "Professor DeLong is one anxious, self-critical soul." I am. Perhaps more to the point, I'm obsessive about analyzing my teaching. As Socrates said, "the unexamined life isn't worth living." I would add that the unexamined teaching life isn't worth continuing.

By examining my teaching continuously, I can identify patterns—patterns that helped me understand my teaching mindset and methods and helped me become better at my profession. I may not be the world's greatest teacher, but I am reasonably self-aware. This self-awareness is a negative and a positive—a negative because it caused me to beat myself up continuously over my real and imagined shortcomings, a positive because it helped me become cognizant of my patterns.

By my mid-thirties, I began to see these patterns emerging not only as a teacher but as a human being. I categorize the patterns in two ways: core and stylistic. The core patterns are deeply embedded in my psyche, and they have significant influence over my most important behaviors and decisions, especially as a professor. The stylistic patterns, as the name suggests, are more surface oriented, affecting everything from how I prepare for the first day of class to how I speak to students. These patterns are neither good nor bad; or, more accurately, they can have good and bad effects. Managing the bad and taking advantage of the good require awareness—awareness that came to me only with teaching experience and maturity. Before examining my growing awareness, let's look at each of these two pattern types in more depth.

Core Patterns

I react to successes and setbacks as either/or experiences; they are either very successful or disastrous. There is never a four or six on a ten-point scale. I either hit a home run or strike out looking on three pitches. After each speech or class or even interaction with a student, I am quick to put a normative value on it. I assess how I did. The more

I recognized this pattern, the better I could manage it. Though this pattern continues to disrupt my life, it would be even worse if I was not aware of it.

Another pattern is a variation on the first. I am pleasant and engaging until I'm not. I respond quickly with too much emotion, sometimes bordering on real anger. I don't seem to be able to respond as an observer and keep perspective in the moment. This pattern arises in the classroom when a student disagrees with me. I can feel my amygdala go into overdrive. My face reddens. The first words out of my mouth are edgy and defensive. I think, "How could this arrogant student push back in class? How could this punk think he knows more than I do?" Finally, I engage in an internal dialogue about how I will dig myself out of the hole I've just created. You see, I've assumed that I am in a hole, instead of envisioning having a symmetric conversation with a friend or colleague or student.

A third pattern relates to risk taking, the pattern I referred to in the previous section. I left a very secure position as a tenured faculty member, as an associate dean at BYU, to join Morgan Stanley; earlier, I headed off to a PhD program when I hadn't been accepted into the program as a twenty-five-year-old graduate student; later, I thought I could travel back to HBS as a thirty-five-year-old who had never taught the case method and begin using it in the middle of the year and teach a course I'd never taught. On the personal side, I initiated a divorce, after twenty-eight years, risking my relationship with my older daughters and going against the strictures of my conservative religion.

This risk-taking pattern has a twist. After I make a big move or do something out of the ordinary, once I land on my feet, I play it safe. It's as if I'm saving up emotional and mental energy for another big risk somewhere down the line. I might take smaller risks in teaching—I might be willing to teach a class I've never taught before—but I'm playing more not to lose than to win. So I've made more dramatic changes than most, but in between these changes, I play it safe.

Not to be overly psychoanalytical, but when I feel like I'm not central to an enterprise, I need to do something that proves I belong. Taking chances in the classroom by teasing students or role playing with drama illustrates that my patterns all possess a high-risk, high-reward outcome, at least in my own mind.

Stylistic Patterns

As a professor, I assiduously avoid lecturing from on high. Instead, my style favors participative classrooms. Early on I realized that show-and-tell was the most important part of the curriculum for kindergarten students. Why would it be any different with adults? Putting voice to thoughts and feelings draws the learner into the process of learning. So I lean on participation for those in the class. I know I can lecture, but to draw out students who may not be engaged and pull them all together as a facilitator has become key to my teaching style.

Another stylistic pattern is that I need to tell stories, as I have already mentioned. My father and mother would tell stories late into the night when we traveled in the car as a family. They were either war stories from my dad's World War II adventures or stories from my mother that related to scary moments she had as a kid. As I reflect on my early teachers, Mr. Stickel and Mr. Snively, I can still recall the hypnotic trance they put me in as I listened to stories about the history of America and the world. Stories enrapture. Stories reach multiple emotions. Stories settle us down and assist us in all getting on the same page, at the same time, in the same room.

A third stylistic pattern is that I like movement in the room. I need to get the atoms colliding, and my pacing creates mental energy. I want students to share this energy and my interest in whatever subject is under discussion. I want us to share conversational intimacy. But most of all, I want to make it personal for them, and when I can move into their space, the conversation becomes more personal. Another benefit: As I move, I gain multiple views of the terrain and the individuals who are involved.

These stylistic patterns manifest themselves in 101 different ways— ways that may seem small initially but in total can affect the classroom environment and my effectiveness in it. As you've seen, these patterns affect how I present myself and material in a classroom.

Now let's look at how I try to manage these patterns and shape my teaching approach to benefit individual students.

THREE

The Worm Deck

Distance Matters

Each day in class is a morality play with those in attendance cast as the actors. This could include visitors (parents, friends of students, visiting faculty), the students, and the teacher. It is the interaction effect that produces the outcomes for each actor in the play. The central actors consist of eighty students who each come with a history consisting of family, geographical location from somewhere around the world, socioeconomic history, family history, work experience, and previous college experience. The case room is divided by concentric rows of students beginning with the sky deck (farthest from the instructor) down to the worm deck (closest to the instructor).

Given all these factors, the classroom gestalt is more complex than it might seem. I try to create a link between what is happening inside my head and my preparation for the day with the biases and assumptions that flow from my history. Just as students have stories from their past that affect their classroom attitudes and performance, so do I. Further, I take into account the intended content to be learned, the context in which it is to be learned, and the students who constitute the actors in the play—this is the essence of teaching.

Ten students are randomly assigned to the worm deck based on previous experience, gender, section assignment, and college history. To bring the morality play to life, I'm going to profile a number of these students and how they ended up at Harvard Business School (HBS). Their combined experiences create an astonishingly diverse environment. This diversity also illustrates how each student can experience the same class moment in very different ways.

Each student brings a different perspective, different abilities, and different experiences to the classroom community, and the cumulative effect can be overwhelming. How do I reach each student? Does each one of them need a different approach on a given day?

I will describe six students who sit in the first row of my class on leadership. Knowing their stories is crucial to me because I want to be able to pay attention to their verbal and nonverbal cues. I want to know each student well enough so that I can respond to all students in a way that meets their emotional and psychological expectations. The students are composites with names changed for obvious reasons.

Andy Andrews

Andy was born and raised in Manchester, England. When I sit in front of the class during a discussion, I find myself sitting closest to Andy. For some reason he's one of my favorites, even though he seems to hate participating in class. When we met and discussed his lack of participation, I realized that he was afraid to speak; he had a faint stutter. He repeated himself often when starting a sentence, and he tripped over the second and third words of his sentences.

I sensed that Andy was very self-contained, even past the point of being an introvert. He smiled at me whenever I looked at him, but the smile hid a fierce intensity that could be glimpsed in his dark brown, piercing eyes. I suspect he felt ongoing stress because of his difficulty speaking in front of the class.

When we met and discussed his participation, he began to explain his background. He mentioned that his family lived meal to meal. Growing up, he attended public schools that were inferior. Andy was also embarrassed by his lack of interest in sports, especially because he attended a school where sports were a major focus. Instead, Andy preferred indoor activities, such as studying maps and reading about places to visit when he graduated from school. He loved music; he played an instrument but couldn't afford renting the instrument during his high school years.

Andy hid his love of numbers when he was growing up. He read books about numbers, about angles, about shapes. He was bored in school with math and so explored the subject on his own and became infatuated with how math worked. His math skills eventually brought him attention. He aced all the tests. He was invited to attend a preparatory school. Though he went to a prep school, he was lonely there and felt out of place everywhere except in the classroom. He arrived at class alone and left alone. He wanted to leave the school but felt like things wouldn't be any better at home. Andy described this time of his life to be traumatic. Once, when I spoke in class about the effects of loneliness, I saw that Andy was crying.

Andy rode his gift of math through college and into investment banking, where he thrived. He was ranked as the top one or two in his analyst class. Even though he did well, Andy wasn't sure if he wanted to return to investment banking because he wasn't sure he fit. He attended HBS for myriad reasons, one of which was to switch careers. He was confident that he could excel in private equity or work in an asset management firm. Yet so far, he hadn't made the cut. No one had to tell him that it was not only that he wasn't a good communicator but that he didn't dress or act like someone who excelled at these alternative finance-related disciplines.

I encouraged Andy through email and personal conversations to engage in class role plays. I know that I was helping him more than I did most other students. Was it because he came from less fortunate circumstances than other students? Was it because he would never be invited to a prestigious Harvard party or gathering? Was it because I saw him as the underdog? Or was it because he struck me as the kind of student I wanted representing HBS? Andy was genuine; he didn't spin his words to win an argument, try to impress, or shade the truth. He was just so real. His clothes were the same every week: simple gray sweatshirt, Levi's, old sneakers. Every week. Over time he began to grow a beard, perhaps to hide more of himself and move toward invisibility. I wasn't sure whether he even liked the class until I invited him to chat with me. It was then, six sessions into the course, that he opined that the course was "frightening" because of how much he was learning about himself; frightening, too, because he realized how unaware he was about his own internal processes and journey. I wondered whether he knew how much I liked him. Was I being unprofessional by favoring Andy over others? Perhaps.

I dealt with Andy with kid gloves. When he spoke in class, I moved toward him, trying to make him feel like we were having a personal conversation. I seldom asked him a follow-up question. I was more concerned about encouraging him. I found myself nodding more in response to what he said, perhaps overcompensating with my nonverbal communication. I didn't care whether students noticed that I slowed down the pace of the discussion when conversing with Andy. I realized early on that I would do whatever it took for Andy to pass my class. *Whatever it took*. I was more invested in some students than in others. This wasn't the first time I grasped that I had favorites.

Nonetheless, I was convinced that no one would know whom I favored. I never am sure when it's going to happen—when I'll develop favorites. It isn't about looks or intellect or charisma or involvement in class. It is about the essence, the soul of the person. Sometimes I encounter kindred spirits; it can be as simple as learning about students from their information cards and something resonates. It's also the feeling I have when I am with them. There is a warmth, a connection. I look forward to individual meetings with these students more than with others. I assume that these individuals sense my interest in their interests, their narrative—but I have no way of knowing if they know how I feel. I try to disguise my favoritism, but how to do so confuses me. It's a natural reaction that other teachers experience, and it's difficult to pretend that I don't have two or three students in each class whom I find particularly compelling. Interestingly, these "favored" students seldom get the best grades in my class. But I know that they get my full attention when they say something in class, when they enter the classroom, when they meet with me.

Catherine McNeely

Catherine made herself known the day she leaned over and teased Michael (her seatmate) for eating too loudly in class. All the students laughed with us as we watched Michael's bright red face get brighter. Catherine seemed more comfortable with who she was than most students. She had a confidence that stopped well short of arrogance. Catherine sat in the last worm deck seat on my right side, facing the classroom. For some reason, I've always felt approaching those sitting close alleviates some nerves and creates less distance; it's probably why I always feel more familiar with the people who sit there. When a male student sat where Catherine was, I often tapped him on his right shoulder (a request for an answer to a question or to respond in some other way) as I passed. But while I was always tempted to do so, I refrained from tapping Catherine. Catherine participated early and often in class.

Catherine had a countenance that was a bit sad, as if she was recovering from a slight or was contemplating some intense experience. She was raised in the Northeast United States in a mixed family (father was Korean, mother American). She described her relationship with her father as being distant and strained. She wanted his approval but felt that she seldom received it. Mom was a "Tiger Mom," affectionate but also ready at moment's notice to push Catherine to achieve all she thought Catherine could achieve. Catherine responded. She attended an Ivy League school, graduated top of her class, and jumped into banking and private equity with both feet. She once told me she felt she had proven to herself she could do the hardest work in New York City. She believed she could compete with anyone. Catherine aspired to qualify for consideration as a Baker Scholar (top 4 percent of graduating students) at HBS. But she hid this drive from most people. She covered it with humor, with a bit of sarcasm, and with the ability to be interested in others.

Early in the semester, I tried to connect with Catherine. She didn't want to make eye contact with me, looking down continuously. She stood six feet tall, and she sat slumped over like she was embarrassed by her height. I was careful not to tease her. I wanted to make some sort of connection with her before pushing her in class the way I thought she should be pushed. I thought she was very smart, but something was getting in her way. I thought I should set up an appointment to meet with her.

What I learned during that appointment was that Catherine wanted a serious relationship more than anything else. She had been "dumped" by two previous guys. She was discouraged that she hadn't seen the signs earlier. She wondered about her naiveté, about her inability to read men, to know what was going on underneath their surfaces. Despite having a lot going for her, Catherine would tear up when she'd talk about wanting to be seriously in love. And she felt time was not on her side, given that she was in the third semester of her four-semester program.

She thought that all the pairing up that took place at the school was complete. She believed the music had stopped and there was no chair for her. There was a feeling of desperation, of resignation. I remember apologizing for all HBS men at one point during a discussion, then backing off. My place and role were to listen. I saw anger, defiance, real mourning. I seldom see this kind of emotion, with that much intensity etched into the face of a student.

All that Catherine had accomplished seemed (to her) for naught. It was as if nothing else counted. The adage that our dreams either make us or destroy us applied to Catherine's mindset. As she left my office for the last time, she made a final comment as I opened the door. She said, "Oh, by the way, I have eight offers. None of them are exploding [the company hiring requires a decision to be made by a certain date, and if a decision can't be made, the offer "explodes" or disintegrates]. I kind of wish a few offers were. The decision-making process would be easier. It would make my decision a lot easier."

Too often students like Catherine dismiss their gifts and focus on where they believe they come up short. Their self-concepts are based on accomplishment. No matter what they accomplish, they discount their achievements and obsess on their self-doubts. They internalize what I call the scarcity model—a conviction that they're missing something. These students believe that if they only had one thing different in their lives, they would be happy. Catherine was a classic example. "If only I was in a committed relationship, my life would be better or perfect or worth living." Or "If only I had a different roommate, I would be more excited about coming home after school."

To help Catherine and others like her become aware of their internalized scarcity models, I suggest they track their internal mind chatter—to notice what they think about, how they feel. I encourage them to become more aware of meta-emotions—how they feel about their feelings. I then walk them through a simple reframing where they talk to themselves about themselves and begin to realize how impossible it is for them to ever achieve their intended goals given the amount of time they have spent focused on their self-doubting dimensions. By making those thoughts and feelings more explicit, students have more choices about how to break their patterns. As they become more conscious of their internal mind chatter, they possess more opportunities to identify and curtail it. It might not happen the first or second time they hear themselves obsessing about their self-doubts, but each time they listen to their internal voice, they have a better chance of doing something about it.

Leonel Pena

Sitting in front of me in the front row in the right-hand seat was Leonel. He had already started two businesses, had one of them go under, and planned on starting two more businesses. But he smiled all the time. He was always the last student to enter the classroom. I could count on Leonel having a mustache of sweat from running across Weeks Bridge, the footbridge that connects HBS with the mother ship, Harvard University. Of course, he'd been running with high-end coffee in his cup.

Once, he asked how he would know whether his current girlfriend was "the one." When he posed this question, I asked him how long they had been dating. "Four years," he said. I asked, "What are you going to learn in the next four years that will change your mind?" Two days later he left me a message that he proposed to his now fiancée.

Leonel attended a prestigious state school. He was proud of his alma mater to the point that he wore paraphernalia from the school most days. He was raised in Miami, but his mother attended HBS. Understandably, Leonel wondered whether he got into the school because of her. This was a recurring theme for him. His parents were very successful, and he couldn't separate what he had earned as opposed to what his parents created for him.

I could depend on Leonel to comment on this identity crisis when we had private conversations. In class, he mused on the state of the world and why he found himself in such a place as HBS. He couldn't seem to confront and acknowledge his past, where he was that day, and where he might end up after school. He felt pressure to take over the family business at some point in the future; he asked himself whether he really had a choice. His constant wrestling with who he was individually versus being a member of his family became his ongoing struggle. And he was not afraid to share it with the class. Perhaps he felt so comfortable talking about these issues because most of the students seemed to know that he came from money. Lots of it. I worried about Leonel, knowing that he did enough worrying for the both of us. I teased him, asking why he hadn't brought his fiancée to class. I could tell I caught him off guard. His face lit up. And the redder it got, the more the class began to laugh at or with him.

From the moment I met Leonel, I knew I could tease him. I felt a kinship with him perhaps because I knew he was a worrier like me. Even though he came from money, he was humble and accepting. I realized that I began most interactions with Leonel in a light, teasing tone. I knew that if I was hard on him, he would perseverate even more about his self-worth versus family worth.

After informing the class about Leonel's fiancée, I returned to my office and received an email from a close friend of Leonel telling me that he hadn't told anyone yet that he was engaged except this close friend and me. Now Leonel had to inform his section, which he didn't want to do until after the holidays. I immediately called Leonel and surprised him with the call. I apologized and expressed regret that I shared something so important to him in an inappropriate way. He laughed and tried to assuage me by saying, "No worries. This will motivate me to send something out tonight to the section."

This incident reminded me how my need to be clever and funny cuts both ways. I question why I need to show off. I question whether or not I need to show the students that I'm "with it." What is it that compels me to use this cutting sense of humor to connect with students? Is it really necessary? What is the desired outcome of teasing students? Don't I remember that time a few years back when a student wrote me the note asking me not to make fun of him in class? Don't I remember that the student was uneasy coming to class knowing that today might be his turn to be teased? How many times does it take for me to learn a lesson? I overstepped my boundaries with little consequence except sending the message that perhaps I can't be trusted after all.

Do we ever know what the consequences of our actions are? I may say something to a student that upsets him, having no knowledge of why a given statement has this effect, since I am not privy to all (or even most) of a student's past experiences. There isn't much to be done about this negative consequence except to have faith in my ability to connect with students, that my genuine interest in them will counter my putting my foot in my mouth inadvertently. A fine line exists between trusting your gut when you talk with a student and trying to change what and how you say it based on certain assumptions. Do you follow your instinct and speak freely to a student, taking a chance that you might say the wrong thing? Or do you tone down your style and actions to avoid the possibility of giving offense?

When I teach such a personal course like Authentic Leadership, the students are particularly sensitive, given that they have shared so much in the weekly learning group sessions. They know that I know much more about them than they know about me. I tone down my use of humor with students when I am dealing with sensitive topics. But it takes a conscious effort on my part to manage my own internal musings in real time—to not say the first thing that pops into my head—so that I create the type of climate where students trust the process of attending class and participating.

Robb Farrell

Picture what a farm boy from Kansas would look like, and you would draw a picture of Robb Farrell. In three different conversations with

Robb, he brought up the pride he had in his family and their commit-ment to one another and to a way of life. He said,

> *I never want to miss a holiday away from my family back home. We have created the family life Norman Rockwell would love to paint. I love our farm, our neighbors [the clos-est neighbor is a half mile away] and the values we live. Pro-fessor DeLong, there have been moments here at HBS where I felt I was in a foreign country. I've seen behavior I've only read about. I didn't really believe people placed their values on hold, let alone my classmates. After a month here I nearly dropped out. Not only did I not fit, but I found myself becom-ing someone I didn't like. I became critical of everyone and everything about this place. My parents began calling every day because they said they were losing their son, that I was changing before their eyes.*

Robb attended a good state school, majored in economics, and joined a consulting firm in Chicago, Illinois. Even though he missed the farm, he enjoyed the intensity of the work and the close ties with other con-sultants. He once commented that completing a project for a CEO on time was like "getting the hay stacked before the storm."

Robb quit the consulting firm after two years when a friend from school called with a startup idea. Robb had been focusing on the tech-nology and software arena at the firm. He'd been obsessed with com-puters since his youth, when he realized that the computer would connect him with a larger world than the farm. He and his friend cre-ated a software product that surpassed their expectations. At the age of twenty-four, Robb found himself sitting on a considerable amount of money, an amount he was too embarrassed to disclose to anyone in his family. In fact, he told no one because he found himself disoriented by this stroke of good fortune.

He and his cofounder ran the company for a year before both applied to HBS. Both were admitted, but only Robb accepted. Robb's colleague felt abandoned and let Robb know it. Arguments and counterarguments ensued. Robb sold his part of the business, and his friend promised that he would never speak to Robb again and would badmouth him to the software community.

As Robb began school, he turned the anger and bitterness from this experience toward his section mates. He mocked them and rolled his eyes when others spoke; he made sarcasm and cynicism his calling cards. Privately, Robb confessed that he was embarrassed by how he behaved after being "thrown to the dogs" by his former friend and partner. He reported that he had settled down and felt like he had resolved his issues by the second year of school. Robb did seem calmer, sometimes a bit depressed. His comments in class were genuine and powerfully vulnerable. I couldn't wait to hear from him during discussions. He was a favorite right from the very first session. I suspect it was because I felt his "type" was underrepresented at school. Hurray for the underdog.

I have an affinity for students like Robb who struggle. I track them more closely than I track others in class. I reach out sooner if I believe they need a boost. Given the priority I place on inclusion, I do everything possible to ensure that they feel included. Robb was a case in point. He felt ill at ease sitting with his classmates. I have built-in radar that tracks those who feel different throughout the class. I ask them softer follow-up questions. I use less humor. I reduce the amount of sarcasm I use with them. I employ supportive gestures and on occasion help them frame their responses. Am I taking psychological liberties by assuming that the students will not be upset that I work harder to help students like Robb? I suppose I'm assuming that students will "get" what I'm doing, that I'm trying to create a psychologically safe zone for all students, that they will trust they're in good hands because I work hard to keep them all safe, even as I also create some classroom discomfort.

Aziz Nasr

Born in the Middle East during a tumultuous time in the world, Aziz lived in fear of receiving a phone call reporting that something had happened to his family. While he was used to the fact that war surrounded him and his family and the accompanying stress and disruption, he possessed a calm demeanor. It had been a while since he had lived near his parents. His first experience in the United States was when he attended Cal Tech in Southern California. He took a job in the energy space before applying and being admitted to HBS.

Aziz admitted that the intersection of business and psychology was new to him. Self-awareness, reflection, journal writing, and sharing internal processes and observations were all foreign activities. After the first session of the course, Aziz walked toward me with an apprehensive look. Sheepish and nervous, he waited until the other students filed out and asked, "Is the class today an example of what it will be like most class periods? Will I have to explore areas of my internal journey any more than I did today? Do I have to tell everything about me?" My reply was simple and to the point: "If you can learn and share like you did today, you will thrive in the class. If you allow your fears to consume you, it will be a nightmare of a course. You should drop it today if you are too frightened. However, some fear and trepidation are expected and encouraged for the growth you expect." Aziz thanked me and slowly walked away. When I studied the add-drop list, he wasn't on it. He remained registered for the course.

Aziz's family had oil money. Lots of it. His father had been an important figure in the oil business in his country. When Aziz spoke of his father, he would lower his voice a bit and be careful with his words. He explained on a number of occasions that he wouldn't ever want to do anything that disappointed his father. At one point during the semester, Aziz called me in a panic because he had been thrown out of a club in downtown Boston and worried that the police would report him to the school. During that particular interchange with Aziz, he talked repeatedly about how he couldn't let his father down. He never referred to his mother. It was as if he didn't have a mother. Aziz felt pressure to return home after graduation but mentioned that he wanted to remain in the United States for five years before returning.

Many students go through crises of various forms. Aziz lived with the chronic worry that his family was in peril. When we communicated outside of class, I told him I was worried whether he was taking care of himself. He never looked rested, and he seemed anxious. I knew him well enough to ask him if he was using drugs. Through these conversations, I began to build a close relationship with him. Perhaps I was the father he wanted. He mentioned on a number of occasions that he never spoke with his parents like he spoke with me. In psychology, transference can refer to patients' directing feelings for a loved one unconsciously to their shrinks. In teaching, a similar phenomenon takes place. It's not just me; other teachers who make the effort to understand and connect with their students sometimes become surrogate parents.

I take advantage of this powerful role. For instance, I encourage students to be more courageous in their communication patterns with everyone. I suggested to Aziz that he ask his parents questions about their histories, about what worried them, about why they made the decisions they did. I have pushed other students to break the patterns of repetitious interactions that added no real content or insights into how they understood one another. I've always believed that conversation is the elixir for enhancing relationships. I try to teach students to communicate on a deeper level if they want to create meaningful relationships. Most of us in our interactions assume we know what the other person will say. It's almost scripted. Many interactions are designed to show how competent we are or that we completely understand the other person. In fact, what if we were curious about others? This curiosity leads to the type of deeper exchanges that builds relationships.

Aziz had turned off authentic communication. However, gradually he began to experience himself differently. He realized that most of his fears were between his ears. He knew by the end of the course that he could begin to manage his internal dialogue. That's when he began to really make significant progress on how he saw others and communicated with them. If I can facilitate this type of breakthrough for a student, then I've done my job a lot better than if I make the student memorize every detail of the case.

Kar-Woon Wang

Kar-Woon took meticulous notes. I could see her notebook as I passed her seat while heading to the board as I responded to a student. There was an intensity to her learning style. Eyes wide open, leaning forward, appearing to hang on every word I spoke, Kar-Woon was my model for the perfect student. She attended HBS after five years in the consumer product business, having learned the ins and outs of that field. She attended a university in Taiwan, followed by more graduate education in Hong Kong. She knew myriad languages well. She seemed confident and authentic. She mentioned numerous times how different this leadership class was in relation to any other course she had ever taken.

At the beginning of class, Kar-Woon mentioned more than once that her culture discouraged any kind of overt conflict in conversation. She said that feelings were to be experienced but not discussed. She highlighted to me how I was challenging her to try new behaviors that ran counter to long-held beliefs and habits learned over many years. I remember mentioning to the whole class on the first day that the processes and skills I was introducing to them were generic enough to cross cultures. I reiterated in our individual meeting this idea of jumping into discomfort even though she was not used to having difficult conversations, for example. I pointed out that the goal of a difficult conversation was to try to understand the point of view of the other person and come to some understanding of how those differences were creating tension between parties. She reluctantly admitted that those skills might be useful in enhancing relationships.

Kar-Woon came into my office a couple of times during the semester to check on how she was doing, whether she was on track in the class and whether she needed to speak more in class. There was a touch of insecurity in her voice, a need for reassurance. She treated me like a deity, which I enjoyed only for the first ten seconds. I needed her to worry less about how she was being experienced and more about what she really wanted and needed from class. As I began class, I would look down at her and ask her if I should begin class. My comment was a way to connect with her and also to tell myself that we were all in this morality play together.

At a certain point I saw an opening with Kar-Woon. I saw an opportunity to ask her in class if she agreed with a comment that another student made that was unexpected and not on point. The comment was a distraction. The comment could have pulled the flow of the class in a different direction. I was forcing Kar-Woon to push back in front of seventy-nine other students.

When I asked her to respond, I spoke softly. I moved up close to her so she would focus on me and not the other students. She took a moment, then said, "I see the situation differently. I see the protagonist as someone who was never clear about direction and focus for the organization." Kar-Woon's comment reflected what I thought most students were thinking and feeling. I asked her to face the student who made the original comment and talk to him. Kar-Woon restated her response looking directly at this student. He argued passionately for his point. Kar-Woon responded with at least equal fervor. It was a great exchange.

After class I emailed Kar-Woon immediately. I told her how proud I was of her efforts and her response. I felt the positive reinforcement would only increase the likelihood that she wouldn't shy away from conflict and instead would engage with others even when a classroom became tense.

The Challenge

I've profiled some of the ten students who were assigned to sit in the front row by the professor, the students whom each semester I get to view up close and personal. Few students want to sit close. They want the freedom of distance from the professor so they can multitask or daydream at a relative remove from the teacher. In the worm deck, they are being observed.

Each student had a narrative, in fact multiple narratives, about how their lives were playing out, whether an outcome was meeting or exceeding expectations. As I studied their faces before and during class, I wanted to know what was really going on in their internal conversations. I knew I had concurrent conversations taking place within me. No doubt, they wanted to know what was going on in my mind. If I would call on a student, we would then have a dialogue between us, meaning that we now had three simultaneous conversations taking place at the same time.

The problem of learning about students, about trying to understand how and why they have ended up in the front row of class, relates to the outcome I have in mind for each one of them and what each of them wants out of the class. How do I take eighty students who have such varied backgrounds and create an environment that generates a few small themes, behaviors, skills, and so on, and allows a degree of freedom for each student to take the material and meld it, chew on it, question it, challenge it, all in the context of his or her own history?

I am compelled to learn about the backgrounds of my students, to understand their drivers and challenges, to recognize who they are as individuals. The people sitting in the worm deck allow me to meet this need. I feel if I know about them, I can listen more intently to what they are saying and feeling. I think there is a higher probability of understanding the multiple levels at which they are processing their individual experiences in the setting of the classroom. To know more about them also informs me how I might be in the moment to respond to their questions and pose questions and at the same time have a sense of how their backgrounds have informed their responses.

I am freer as a teacher if I feel I know the students on some level, better able to adjust and adapt to their requirements. I will expect them to begin to share at least some of their internal stories with the class and in their learning groups more than superficial, biographical data that could have been found on their student cards. I also want the students to know that I care about them enough to understand who they are and how they live their lives at a complex and trying time for many of them. My hope is to turn their mindset from one of certainty to curiosity where their assumptions can be tested, confirmed, or revealed to be false.

FOUR

Teaching Individuals

Trying to Create an Equal Opportunity Classroom

As the last chapter suggests, every student is unique, and teachers must consider the needs of particular students as well as the group's desired goals. The biggest challenge with individuals, however, is if you've been teaching for a while, you start categorizing students reflexively. Over thirty-five years of teaching has informed me, whether for good or for ill, that certain types of students exist. For instance, some are enthusiastic about the course initially and then lose interest. There are also students who communicate that they already know the material, looking down on me and others who might be wasting their time. Some students struggle with the requirement to participate in class. There's always a student who knows he should participate but continues to self-criticize as the class progresses.

A related statistical phenomenon also affects the ability of teachers to focus on individuals. In a class of eighty students, a natural distribution of students exists in which a small percentage will perform above and below the mean. The questions that I and every teacher face are,

To whom are we teaching? Are you teaching to the ten smartest students or the ten who are falling behind? I find myself worrying about the students at the far ends of the continuum and assume that those who are in the middle will take care of themselves.

I want to make the class rigorous enough for those who take to the course and excel, whether because of their effort or natural abilities. I don't want them to be bored, act bored, or send implicit or explicit messages that the course and the content are soft. There will also be those students who haven't thought about the human dimension and the multilayered facets of human behavior. It is just as problematic to have a small number of students who always look like they are in a fog, trying to understand what a cognitive distortion is or what heuristics mean. If I'm worrying about these individuals at either end of the continuum, what happens to those who live in the mean?

To address those students who are in the statistical middle, I hold in-class simulations and exercises to assess student abilities and to mentor real time in class. In this way, I can pay more attention to those who might otherwise escape my notice. Before class, I ask myself whether I've created a curriculum and class plan that will attend to the needs of all the students. I try to make sure that the class doesn't go over the heads of even a few. I hope to have the material just hard enough to keep the students engaged. I keep reminding myself not to forget those in the middle. Through eye contact, quiet conversations throughout class with students, and constant attention to the spirit of the class, I increase the probability of paying attention to all students regardless of interest or academic ability.

But there are other obstacles to the ideal of creating a class that addresses the needs of all students equally. Over the course of my career, I've found it useful to keep the following three tendencies in mind:

- Playing favorites
- Prejudging
- Classifying

I do each of these activities reflexively, and sometimes they hurt my ability to be fair to all. But by being aware of each of these reflexive actions, I can sometimes do a better job of focusing on the individual needs of students. Let's examine each and how they affect the classroom.

Favorites

Let's be honest. I believe that every professor has favorite students. Yet somehow I convinced myself that no student would be able to tell. I counted on my opacity—my teacher's mask of objective professionalism—to hide that I preferred one student over another. For years, though, I've had students whom I liked more than others. I still can't figure out not only why I prefer one student over others but with whom it is going to happen. It isn't about intellect or looks or charisma or quantity of participation in class. It is about the essence, the soul of the person. The ones I favor feel like kindred spirits even when I don't know anything about them beyond what I've gleaned from their student information cards. It's the feeling I have when I am with them. There is a warmth, a connection that is difficult to define.

I look forward to individual meetings with favorite students more than I care to confess. I'm sure that students feel my interest in their interests, their narrative. If they don't sense my concern, I will be frustrated. And I have no way of knowing if they know how I feel. I recognize that I need to hide who my favorites are, yet how I do so confuses me. The two or three students in each class who are my favorites seldom get the best grades; I don't grade unfairly based on my personal preferences. But I know that they get my full attention when they say something in class, when they enter the classroom, when they meet with me.

Prejudging Students

Every faculty member begins to create a biography, a narrative, for each student. Even with little information at hand, we still are confident in our ability to understand students, to relate with them, to know what is going on in their other lives. This is another paradox: Regardless of how many times I've been dead wrong in assessing the psychological state of my students, I have not lost confidence in my ability to understand all of them all the time. My sense is that this belief is as true as the belief that most men have that they are good drivers. There is no evidence, but the belief still exists.

It's not just this belief that I understand them that leads to prejudging; it's the simple, human fact that I like some students more than I like others. I like some immediately the first time I'm in their presence, before they've said a thing. There is no consistent pattern in these feelings for students. It has nothing to do with students' being brilliant, or from foreign lands, from prestigious schools, or other characteristics. As I write this, I am realizing that I do have a bias toward students from rural areas. I always want to give them the benefit of the doubt, and maybe it has to do with my preference for students who are less elegant in their language skills. And I like students more if they feel entitled or arrogant.

On the other hand, I have found myself rooting against the students I don't like. On more than one occasion, I've thought, "I hope his comment is lousy so that he will be one step closer to getting a poor grade. After all, I need to force rank the students, and why not have one of the lower 10 percent of the class be him?" I also have to make an effort to listen and empathize with their "high-end" world experiences such as bungee jumping over alligator-infested waters and then chilling out at five-star hotels.

Given the way I was raised and my experiences, I'm suspicious of students I perceive are wealthy because I believe they didn't earn their way through life. I realize this reaction is a commentary on me, on my history and my experiences. But teachers should be aware of how their own backgrounds and biases affect their views of students.

Your history, your family, and the context in which you have experienced life inform the way you create eighty different student narratives. I've confessed my likes and dislikes to make a point about the challenging situation in which teachers find themselves. As long as I remain confident that I possess superhuman powers of ESP, the spirit, the security, and the risk taking within the walls of the classroom will constantly hang in the balance. Not only will my ability to reach as many students as possible be affected, but the students will intuit and interpret my every movement, trying to decipher my intentions, my authenticity, my motives, and my heart. All this psychological back and forth can be taxing. The last thing I want is to have students worry about their respective relationship with me or with others in the classroom. They shouldn't be worrying whether I like them or not. It's natural for every student and teacher to lose concentration during the course of a class. However, students need to feel secure in their feelings about how I perceive them and my interest in them. They needn't waste emotional energy on whether or not they are a favorite or who might be my favorite students.

Given that I know these imperfections in my personality, my psychological makeup, what advice and counsel do I have for myself and for others who on occasion judge students before all the evidence is in? First, follow the lessons taught in Alcoholics Anonymous or any other addiction-related treatment process. Get back on track and forgive yourself and others by admitting that you are normal and that you can be different. Ask for support from other faculty whom you trust and respect. Know yourself well enough to know when you are most judgmental. Is it earlier in the day? Is it later in the semester when you are searching for different ways to evaluate students? Is it when you are less prepared?

What disappoints me the most about some of my evaluative judgments is how sure I am early in the semester that I have a sense of a student's "essence." I remember a student whom I approached on the first day of class, asking him why he was taking the course. He told me that it fit his schedule so that he could have classes early in the week. I found myself recoiling, distancing myself from the student. Should I tell him that he is taking up the seat of someone who cares more about the class than he does? Instead, I shut down our conversation and moved on to another student.

I realized I wanted validation from students to deal with my anxieties at the beginning of a course. I wanted them to tell me how much they were looking forward to the class. I wanted them to tell me they listed the course in the selection process as their number one choice. The student who was honest with me about his desire for another early course had an uphill battle to win me over. Judgment was set. He had to prove to me that he was worthy of my efforts. He had to prove to me that he deserved my attention and the attention of the other students.

Students have shown up late on the first day, and I immediately made judgments without knowing anything about them other than their names and that they were in their second year. They could have been in an accident on the way to school. They could have been caring for sick children or had some other legitimate extenuating circumstance, but I will have none of that thinking cloud my preconceived notions. What is alarming is that I've been teaching for over thirty-five years. I should know better. While I'm more aware of these tendencies than when I was less experienced, they continue to affect my judgments. Still, I hope they affect my judgments now less than in the past because of this self-awareness.

I've emphasized the importance of knowing your patterns, since such knowledge fosters heightened self-awareness, and I believe it can moderate this judging tendency. Here's what I'd advise every teacher to do: List those characteristics you bring into the classroom that allow you and the students to create a unique place to learn. Here's my list:

- Memorizing every student's name and background.

- Building sufficient trust through my interactions with students that they want to seek counsel during office hours.

- Fostering a sense of classroom excitement and using narratives that results in rapt attention most of the time. The attendance in my classes is consistently 100 percent.

- Demonstrating my care for and concern about the success of each student. Each semester a number of students write that they have never met another professor who they believe is more committed to them.

What also helps me move away from judging students unfairly or prematurely is focusing on the classroom topic through conscious agenda setting. Even when I'm tempted to judge, I remind myself of my patterns, and this helps me toward a spirit of fairness and appreciation. And even when I feel "centered" and in good shape to teach, I try to see myself from a third person's perspective. Can I disassociate myself from myself and view Professor DeLong from a corner of the classroom, observing how the professor is interacting with the students? Do I have the ability to have conversations with myself about what is going on in the classroom in real time?

When I find myself evaluating students on behaviors that I don't understand, I will quickly assume something is wrong or that a student is not involved in or committed to the class. If I see a student who I believe is daydreaming, I often assume disinterest from the student. I typically don't give the student the benefit of the doubt. It is part of the human experience to judge behavior or communications that we don't understand. We seldom give one another the benefit of the doubt if we don't understand the situation or context. We quickly leap to judgment. Go easy on judgment. Be more curious than certain of what you see and perceive.

Classifying

Now let's examine four common student types, and how these types affect my classroom demeanor and behavior toward these categorized students.

The Frightened Student

The farther I stand in the classroom from the student who is struggling with participation, the harder it seems to be for the student to focus. Standing too close can cause anxieties as well. One of the ways I've determined whether a student is struggling with participation is not only through past participation patterns but in observing the student's body positioning—whether the student seems relaxed or stressed, appears frightened, is chatting before class begins, or is sitting silently alone. I ask myself the following questions:

- When the student walks into the class, is he alone?

- Does she make small talk with others as she walks across the class or up the rows to her seat?

- Does it feel like the student is walking to an execution rather than to a class to learn?

- Is the student willing to make eye contact with me, or does he avoid it at all costs, fearing even to smile because I might interpret his smiling as permission to call on him in class?

I have a strategy for dealing with frightened students. First and foremost, I understand that many college environments are competitive and filled with judgments. Even though the student has attended classes before, I acknowledge that this student has not been in this situation before. However, if the student makes no contact with anyone, I worry that fear is at the core of the situation. But in my efforts to encourage the student, I can put added pressure on her if I try too hard. It would be like speaking too slowly or loudly to someone who doesn't seem to understand English well; these actions communicate that I consider this individual handicapped. I would embarrass and create more self-consciousness in this student. The best thing I can do is listen as hard as I can. I need to determine whether or not the student is making eye contact with me. Is her skin splotchy? Is the breathing occurring from the neck up? Are the hands on the desk? Are they shaking? Is the student mumbling and struggling with articulating a thoughtful idea? I often begin to breathe very deliberately, from the stomach. I breathe slowly. I smile warmly at the person and nod encouragement. I want the students to know I'm pulling for them every way I know how to support them.

When I believe a student is frightened, I move about a yard away from this individual. I talk in a less commanding, less authoritative tone of voice. I want to turn the experience into a conversation between the two of us rather than a lecture or an inquisition. I may intentionally ask the student a less complex question based on a value judgment rather than the case facts. I don't lock eyes with the student but show passive interest while listening, since a direct stare can be intimidating. I give nods where appropriate. I slow down my cadence to create a more relaxed atmosphere. I'm like Goldilocks: not too close and not too far. If the respondent's answers are poor and he knows it, I don't linger. I move on. I want to distract rather quickly and engage with someone else.

But I will circle back around spatially to the student. For example, if the student is sitting on an aisle, I may stand by him later in the session and tap him on the arm deftly so that I communicate commitment to him and to our relationship.

All my opinions and suggestions about classroom positioning and demeanor apply doubly to younger faculty members. Don't expect to be great at managing the content, the atmosphere, your boards, or your own state of mind with the grace and expertise of the seasoned teacher. Practice is crucial to teaching. As you experiment with your own comfort with physical distance from students in the classroom, know that the students will give you the benefit of the doubt as you try a few different approaches. Most important, be aware of how intervention with a frightened student is proceeding and whether you are getting traction in the process. It is your self-awareness and self-regulation in real time that will transform your experience and the experiences of the students from disasters to memorable moments of harmony.

Will I ever feel comfortable turning my back on some of the students and focusing on the students located on the other side of the room? Why is it that the closer I get to the students, the quieter I find myself speaking? My voice can turn into a whisper. Why do I find myself walking up the aisle where the student who questions my authority is sitting?

The Self-Assured Student

Students who attend graduate school are assumed to be self-assured enough to hold their own in classroom discussion. However, each student brings to the classroom tendencies, habits, and preferences for participating in class discussion. The challenge is that HBS students know that half their grade will be weighted based on participation in class. Most faculty members will ask the questions, "How has this student enhanced the discussion? How has this student brought the class to a different way of thinking?" Ten percent of the students attend the school to help them get over their fear of speaking in front of groups. They know they need to be forced into speaking. Thus, they put themselves into this type of situation.

However, some students are simply more extroverted, and they've learned how to survive and thrive through classroom participation. They have also learned that it's better to create the illusion of competence by speaking up early and often. A number of the students feel confident speaking among their peers regardless of whether they know what they are saying or the quality of what is being said. Yet, they still feel they have a right to express their opinions or are entitled to air time. They are often experienced at jumping into situations where they get by with their wits rather than with their wisdom.

The other class members teach me through their behavior whether an overly self-assured student is rubbing us all the wrong way. When it feels like the student is preaching or "acting all knowing," I find myself veering toward my pattern of getting angry. My internal dialogue goes something like, "Do you think I was born yesterday? Can't you see that you are embarrassing yourself? How did you get through the first year of courses behaving like an arrogant jerk? What makes you think I can't read my students?" I'm exacerbating the problem if other students know that I'm letting the overly self-assured student get to me.

What is the instructor to do with the student who wants to participate on most queries—the one who raises his hand first and may even wave it like a flag to get your attention? What do you do with the student who creates the illusion of complete confidence with the material and the context? As I write this, I need to differentiate between the arrogant student and the one who is overly eager to participate. The latter is an easier task, better handled in a one-to-one conversation. When I explain my appreciation for the student's enthusiasm in the course, I also remind her that I need to involve all ninety students throughout the semester, that my role is like an orchestra director. If only one instrument and one player are highlighted in every piece, the orchestral sound will suffer. Instead, the conductor must make sure that all the musicians feel that they're getting their chance to shine, and that different instruments are featured in accordance with the piece being played.

The apparently arrogant student also needs individual attention, but this is more of a challenge. The initial reaction by the instructor might be to "put the student in his place." This can be accomplished by intimidating the student, embarrassing him, or trying to trap the student with content nuances. However, these approaches never work long term. Most student communities are self-regulating; the students themselves keep a lid on arrogant classroom behaviors through teasing, mimicking, or talking straight about the observed behaviors. If these norms don't exist, I speak individually to the student and express my observations. I hope that the student is coming to class. I also use silence so that I don't find myself lecturing or talking too much due to my own apprehension or nervousness in giving the student feedback about his irritatingly arrogant demeanor.

When a faculty member does give direct feedback to arrogant students, the tendency is for the faculty member to talk faster, louder, and longer. However, most faculty members don't believe they need to give such direct feedback. One approach might be to simply state what you've observed, see how the student responds, and plan with the student what the next steps might be. An example might be, "Roger, sometimes when you respond, you say it in a way that makes it sound like you are sure you're the only student with a valid comment. There is a tone in your voice that makes it sound like you are lecturing the class instead of putting forth an idea that is your opinion and not the only answer to the question."

Enlist the student by inviting him to help solve the dilemma if indeed he feels motivated to do so. For example, one could say to a student, "I've observed a certain behavior when you respond to a question or when you respond to another class member. At some point I'd be happy to share those observations." There also isn't a need for humblebragging by stating, "I may be all wrong, but I've noticed something you might be interested in." Why wouldn't I take the time to share a perception whether it's positive or negative?

The Comic

Some students become nervous when the tensions are too great in a class. That nervous energy prompts them to make a funny comment, a wisecrack, to relieve the tension in the room. Silence is important in teaching. In the first-year required curriculum, there will be those who only know how to respond to this environment with comic relief. It gets tiring after a time. However, these students become stuck in a pattern of communicating that probably began when they were kids.

It may have worked. But if you believe that a particular student will always try to bring humor and lightness to a teaching moment, consider chatting with that student. Challenging the student to enlarge the student's repertoire of replies in the class is an option. Speak quietly to the person offline. I've embarrassed too many students by trying to "out-cute" them with sarcasm. It's a dangerous game. Having a heart-to-heart conversation off line will enhance your relationship with the student.

The danger in not having the conversation is that over time students will expect a joke or some levity whenever the particular student makes a comment. Simply by calling on the person, I have made a decision that it's OK for laughter or it's OK for a lighter touch. I become boxed in myself because I haven't previously chatted with the student. No matter what is taking place in the class, by calling on the person, I've signaled to the whole class that I want comic relief.

Another reason to talk with the student is to disrupt a pattern that doesn't allow any other response by the student. The student doesn't know how to do anything else because of the expectations that exist that he will say something that is intended to be clever or comical. Disrupt the pattern sooner rather than later. The longer a teacher waits to chat about perceptions of a "funny" student, the less students will respond the way they believe they are supposed to behave. Over time I've now set the expectation that I want an interlude from the direction I'm taking the class. Help the student out by dealing with the behavior before everyone is stuck in a dysfunctional pattern.

The I'm-Not-Ready-for-Prime-Time Student

Some students aren't prepared for class, don't do the work acceptably, and appear disengaged and disinterested. This doesn't happen just once but is repeated behavior. As the evaluator of my students, I have a responsibility to assess how much they have learned in class. I have a responsibility to guide and direct ninety students as a collective, as a community. (I'll use different class sizes throughout to represent varying class sizes based on class subject.) Yet there are individual requirements for passing the course where each student must illustrate to me that he can meet the expectations of the requirements of the course. If a student is ill-prepared once or at the most twice, I will speak to that person outside the classroom. I might say something like, "Is everything OK? You mentioned to me last week you weren't prepared. How can I help?" I might add, "I look forward to having you all in for the course. If there are extenuating circumstances, let's talk about it. But if it's something else, we should talk more."

If I query whether the student is really in the game or interested in the game and she says "no," I ask if she could help me understand what's going on. If she is blunt with her feedback, I express my appreciation that she's shared the data. Every student has the right to sign on at the beginning of the course and sign off at any moment. I might make an arrangement with the student, requesting that she at least look like she's engaged and committed to the course, even if she isn't. If it's early in the semester, I might ask the student whether he needs to drop the course. I might tell the student that I've been noticing that he rolls his eyes in class when others speak. I explain that it makes me uncomfortable because I'm worried about the effect on the person speaking and I'm worried about him. I might even invite the person to not come to class. But I remind myself to say it in a way that isn't condescending or punishing or vengeful. It may only take a raised eyebrow or a smirk on my face that communicates that I don't believe what the student is saying—or worse, that the student isn't worthy of my time and energy.

The Conscious Classroom

Just as you can learn by rote, you can teach by rote. This is a danger for veteran teachers, who may operate almost on autopilot, relying on teaching methods and materials that they used repeatedly over the years. To a certain extent, most teachers repeat what works, and that's fine until they start going through the motions. This is especially problematic when it comes to students.

These teachers are especially vulnerable to the behaviors I've described: prejudging, playing favorites, and classifying. As I've described, I'm acutely aware of these behaviors. Being conscious of them is a good way to keep them under control.

We're all human, and we're never going to eliminate these behaviors entirely. The goal should be to manage them. The best teachers don't let their prejudging get in the way of their final judgments of students, they try to treat favorites and nonfavorites the same, and they are aware that their classifying reflex may be causing them to view a unique person in stereotypical ways.

It just takes a commitment to teaching consciously to prevent these tendencies from diminishing student receptivity to learning.

FIVE

The Ties That Bind

Covenant versus Contractual Relationships

Covenants are crucial in teaching. They create bonds of trust and faith that facilitate learning and growth. This is as opposed to contractual relationships, where people interact on a purely transactional basis— that is, students study to pass the course and receive good grades. When a covenant exists, however, it can transform relationships.

Up to this point, I've focused primarily on teaching, but as I've indicated earlier, the intersection between teaching and leadership can be instructive. Every so often, I'm going to examine this intersection. When the subject is covenants, I am compelled to look at their value from the perspective of both leaders and teachers. I think teachers can learn a lot by examining what happens when leaders form powerful covenants with their employees as well as the negative consequences of purely contractual relationships.

Before looking at covenants and contractual relationships, though, let's examine the parallels between leaders and teachers. Once you see the similarities between these two professions—similarities that may not be obvious at first glance—the discussion of covenants and contracts will be that much more meaningful.

Different Jobs, Similar Challenges

I'm always surprised that people don't see the connection between teachers and business leaders, but perhaps that's because most people haven't experienced both roles. Because of my experiences at Morgan Stanley and as a teacher—and because I tend to obsess about these types of things—I've become aware of the remarkable similarities. Before working at Morgan Stanley, I struggled to find the most effective way to run a class. Afterward, I found that I could draw on my experiences and apply them to teaching. I had an advantage that most teachers lack: I had been a business leader, and I could translate lessons learned at a company to the classroom.

The best leaders and teachers listen deeply, communicate empathically, and motivate adroitly. Command-and-control leaders and strict, punishment-wielding teachers are stereotypes of the past. Today, leaders and teachers need to relate to their audiences, influencing actions rather than dictating them. Both must be brave enough to make themselves vulnerable and admit mistakes.

In addition, teachers lead and leaders teach. Again, this may not be obvious, but think about how teachers model behaviors they want students to adopt, how they motivate by telling stories, how they make decisions that affect all students. Similarly, leaders have become teachers in knowledge-centric environments; they can't just tell people what to do but must help them acquire ideas, information, and skills so they can be more innovative, agile employees. Like teachers, leaders mentor. This is a role that has gained a lot of importance in recent years.

Finally, the best teachers and leaders build relationships. As organizations have flattened and moved away from the pyramid model, leaders have recognized the value of relationship building. When leaders create meaningful relationships with their people, they also create loyalty and an environment where employees feel secure enough to take chances and suggest innovative and sometimes disruptive ideas. Teachers, too, have learned that they shouldn't just be "talking at" students but talking with them. Creating trust and helping students learn and grow are critical teacher responsibilities.

With these parallels in mind, let's focus on the related but somewhat different tasks of leaders and the value of covenants in the performance of these tasks.

How Leaders Create Covenants

When I speak of leadership, I'm referring to the process of bringing others together and accomplishing three central tasks. The first role of the leader is to set direction. Humans are born goal directed. They want to move forward. Most become antsy or anxious when they lack direction. Ultimately, if there is no direction over an extended period of time, they can shut down and become isolated.

But with direction, ordinary people can accomplish extraordinary things. That is the magic of bringing people together and witnessing them accomplishing goals. First, leaders must articulate a direction and involve their people in creating the direction.

Second, leaders must create buy-in or commitment to the direction. This is no small feat. The process of getting humans to commit sounds rather simple, but the reality can be challenging. This is a critical task; if commitment is absent, there is little to no chance to accomplish the task at hand. When this lack of commitment affects hundreds or thousands of employees, entire organizations vanish. The vanishing act cannot be blamed solely on competitive forces. Most organizations that self-destruct experience failure because employees were not committed to the mission and direction of the organization.

Harvard University didn't self-destruct when it had a leader who struggled with this role, but it certainly foundered during this time. Larry Summers, former secretary of the US Treasury and president of Harvard University, was consistently the smartest person in the room. He relished being at the top of the heap of intellectuals. His leadership style at Harvard seemed to revolve around outwitting the faculty and staff and alumni. It felt like he was leading with his head and not with his heart and soul. He established little connection with his constituency. It was only a matter of time before the faculty turned on him, exhibiting no loyalty. Summers ultimately received a vote of no confidence because he engendered no commitment.

Third, leaders must facilitate execution or implementation. By facilitating execution, leaders drive growth and innovation. While some leaders define themselves by how much they accomplish, they don't always get employees on board when it comes to getting things done. They may be great strategists and come up with terrific ideas, but if they fail to engage their people in implementation tasks, they'll come up short, as will their people.

All three of these elements are unwritten promises leaders make to their people: *I promise to set direction with you, to secure your commitment, and to help you execute. If I do these things, you'll succeed and so will the company.* This is the covenant leaders establish with their employees, and it drives performance far better than salary and perks.

Leaders seal this covenant personally. The kind of person you are matters. The kind of environment you create matters. The kind of relationships you forge matters. In reality, the art and practice of leadership are deeply personal for the leader and those being led. They are deeply personal because molecules are stirred when a leader has an interaction with another person. Energy is transmitted. Something transpires between two humans.

The odds are that some of you have never worked for a business or led a company. But I'm asking you to imagine that you have this job and answer the following three categories of questions:

1. Do you have a philosophy about how you experience other people? What are your beliefs about how humans are motivated? Are extrinsic or intrinsic rewards more important? Do you trust others? Do you believe that humans naturally want to work, or do they need to be supervised in order to ensure they don't become lazy or slack off? Entering relationships with certain types of beliefs about motivation informs the degree of intimacy and honesty in these relationships. It will impact how you work in teams, how you strategize and organize the work; it will determine how well you as a leader can leverage the employees of the enterprise.

2. How do others experience you? How open are you to feedback? How curious are you about how your behavior helps or hinders others? Do employees spend countless hours hiding the truth from you or figuring out what to say in order to please you? Leaders need multiple mirrors that tell them if they're doing a good job or if they need to develop themselves further.

3. How sensitive are you to what is happening inside other people when they are in your presence? What is happening emotionally and psychologically when you interact with other people? Are you an instrument for fundamental change?

In your imagined leadership role, you may be responsible for hundreds or even thousands of other people—a lot more employees than the number of students that you have in a classroom. You may have risen through the corporate ranks because of your financial brilliance or your sales acumen or your technological savvy. But as you reviewed these questions, you realize that they're about people and perceptions—how you perceive others and how they perceive you. Your responses to these questions determine whether you can form covenant relationships with your people. They reflect your ability to do what leaders today must do—set direction, create commitment, and execute—and do it on much more of a covenant than a contractual basis.

Let's segue to how teachers create covenants with students, and I think you'll see the parallels with leadership.

How Teachers Create Covenants

This is a subject about which I'm passionate, and so I trust you'll indulge me personalizing aspects of the covenant-creation process.

From the first moment in the classroom, the teacher is laying the groundwork to create a covenant with students—a relationship where the student develops faith in the teacher and the teacher reciprocates with trust-based connections to students. I hope to create an environment where students know I care about them, or at the very minimum know that I care about them by extension. My love of my subject and my preparation extends to them. But I must convince them that I care and am committed to them.

Why do I want to create a covenantal relationship? Does it make a difference? Let's look at why it matters and what a covenant means. As you'll discover, a number of parallels exist between the covenant leaders establish and how the best teachers teach.

Here are the three dimensions of building a covenantal relationship in the classroom.

First, students must know that they are in safe, competent, understanding hands. The first dimension is built on faith. I want students to have faith in the process that over time increases in excitement and in density. I want students to know that I'm thinking about the class night and day, that it's my top priority. They must feel secure when they walk into the classroom. They must feel secure as they fulfill class assignments outside of class.

Second, students need to know that teachers care about them and their work. They learn this through feedback, interactions in the classroom, and observing them interact with their peers. I strive to help my students feel it as we chat one-to-one in my office or anywhere on campus.

Third, students must feel like they are learning and growing and developing. They need to know that they are being stretched and pushed and challenged with new knowledge, that their assumptions are being tested, and they must gain new knowledge about themselves.

This three-dimensional approach guides me as I prepare and develop classroom materials as well as when I teach. The students expect it, and I expect it of myself. Recall our discussion of leaders, and you can see that all of this translates to what employees hope to receive from their bosses. Though there are obvious differences because of the environment (classroom versus office) and financial relationship (students pay school; company pays employees), the need for empathy, insight, and opportunities for learning and development are remarkably similar.

What's the Difference between a Covenant and a Contractual Relationship?

As you think about these covenant relationships, you might be wondering about the contractual opposite. Though I stated the basic difference earlier—the latter is transactional; the former is based on faith and truth—it's worth exploring the differences between these two types in more detail.

In a covenant, leaders and teachers are "all in." They concentrate on connecting with each employee or student so that each person believes he or she can be successful. "Best self" means arriving with an attitude that is aspirational and focused on possibilities.

Leaders and teachers show up to work thinking of others as much as or more than they do of themselves. They help foster an inclusive mindset, focused on making the whole team or class better. They balance the interests of the group and each professional or student. But here's the key difference from a contractual relationship: they are generous in the ways they meet the objectives of others.

In a contractual relationship, leaders and teachers show up to fulfill their obligations from a purely cognitive standpoint; they have no emotional skin in the game. They are only focused on individual objectives. They possess a survival mentality, assuming they are in the service of self. They may very well feel that they are marking time until something better comes along. They focus on looking busy or worse, taking credit where credit isn't due.

Contractual leaders and teachers worry about their image, how they are perceived by their boss—a manager or department head. They possess little empathy for others because their goal is to survive where they perceive themselves to be unwelcome. Psychologically speaking, they are turning inward in an effort to have enough energy to see alternatives where they will feel valued and part of the larger group. But the irony is that the more they worry about their own image, the farther the distance created from others and self.

When teachers and leaders are focused on purely transactional relationships, they become cynical and believe that any alternative is better than the current situation. More important, they become disconnected from universities and companies. In their cynical minds, someone else is to blame for their disconnection and dissatisfaction. They may demonize their bosses, their institutions, and their students and employees.

In covenants, on the other hand, leaders and teachers are concerned about all employees and students, not just the best and the brightest. They are especially worried about those who feel lost and disoriented. They may not be able to "save" everyone, but they make an attempt to develop their employees and help their students learn and grow, no matter the abilities or achievements of their employees or students.

Finally, leaders and teachers who have contractual relationships endanger their organizations, while those with covenants fortify them. Contractual leaders and teachers create low morale—students and employees don't perform up to their capabilities. Contractual leaders and teachers fail to inspire students and employees to shoot higher, and they fail to instruct them how to do so; they settle for mediocrity. Those who embrace covenants are great motivators; they are also conscientious about fulfilling their obligations to students and employees. When those who embrace covenants make a promise, they try to keep it.

Covenants Can Be Fragile

Teachers and leaders have only a limited amount of time with students and employees. If leaders and teachers establish trust-based covenants with their charges, great learning will take place. I want the students to feel committed to the content and the process of my class, not just cognitively but affectively. Why waste time if students show up with expectations of having only an intellectual experience? I want them to be all in, just as leaders expect the same commitment from their employees. The goal is for employees and students to show up to work and school with head, heart, and soul. They are fully present. They feel like they are integral to the business and academic experience.

This won't happen unless the covenant is nurtured and reinforced continuously. It's not a onetime event, like signing a contract. Covenants are only as strong as the commitment of the people making them. Teachers and leaders must feel a responsibility to keep relationships strong, not only to achieve good outcomes for the individuals and the institutions but because they're motivated intrinsically to help those who are in their classrooms and offices.

To grasp both the value and the fragility of this covenant, let's look at what happens when the student *feels* as if the covenant has been broken (I emphasized that word because appearance may not be reality; the covenant may only seem broken because of a student's perception).

Let's say that the teacher cancels a meeting with a student, Lauren, because the teacher tells her that he will be out of town. During the time the appointment had been scheduled, Lauren goes to the gym and observes the teacher working out.

Lauren begins to feel anger, resentment, frustration. She needs some advice from this particular teacher by week's end and it's now Wednesday. Lauren moves quickly past the door to the weight room because she doesn't want to embarrass herself or her teacher. Yet she somehow wants to communicate to the teacher that he was "caught." Lauren continues to reflect on why the teacher would have lied to her. Why would he be so obvious in his white lie?

By the time Lauren leaves the gym, she has concluded that the teacher doesn't like her, that the teacher didn't like her comment in the previous class, that the teacher is planning on giving her a poor grade in class, that the teacher has been making up stories and lying to students through the semester, and that the teacher shouldn't be teaching a course on authentic leadership. Basically, Lauren has written the teacher off, and the trust that should exist has vanished.

Regardless, if there are two sides to this story, Lauren has created her version from this experience. The teacher doesn't know Lauren was at the gym, and she doesn't think he saw her. But what if they were aware of each other's presence? Should she approach and confront him? Should she wait and have him approach her, assuming he saw her? Should she write him an email or a note about this incident or just forget it?

What about the teacher? Does it matter that he canceled his trip and spent the morning with his wife who was being treated for cancer? Does it matter that the teacher was upset after seeing the pain his partner was in and needed a physical workout to deal with that emotional upset? Did he have an obligation to call Lauren and meet with her now that he wasn't traveling? Did he have an obligation to tell Lauren about the situation with his wife?

This example illustrates how a covenantal relationship can move from commitment to distrust because of one incident. In most situations like

I've described, the teacher or student isn't going to follow up and clear the air by sharing his or her story. Now, when Lauren attends class the next class period, she is feeling more detached, less interested in participating, more guarded, less trusting. She feels remote internally, and this feeling manifests itself externally.

Everything we do as teachers is either adding to or detracting from the emotional bank account we build up in our relationships. Even if our students possess a spirit of generosity, there are moments that call into question the relationship. This happens in every relationship. Some event can set the table for trouble.

It's Not That We Break Covenants Intentionally...

As Lauren's story indicates, misperceptions can endanger covenants. But the best leaders and teachers are aware of the different factors that can weaken a covenant's bonds. Here are two examples.

George, a university professor, was conducting a graduate seminar when one of his favorite students, Lucas, challenged him on a point he was making about a text they were reading. George had always encouraged his students to feel free to disagree with him, and in the past, he had usually responded to these disagreements logically and fairly. But this time, George responded by tearing into Lucas. Not only did he become angry and assault Lucas's reasoning and ability to understand what they were studying, but he suggested that Lucas tended to speak before he thought, and that this was a good illustration of "your character flaw." Lucas's face turned red when George criticized him and his voice shook when he tried to apologize.

Later, George was aghast at his classroom behavior. He knew that he had responded the way he had in part because he was in a lousy mood—he'd had an argument with his wife that morning and he'd just heard that he'd been turned down for a grant for which he had applied. But that was no excuse for embarrassing a student—a student who was smart and talented and who George liked a lot—with his mean-spirited remarks. George had broken the covenant between himself and Lucas, and Lucas would never forget it or be willing to trust George again.

Like George, I'm haunted by the moments when I've broken the covenant with students. To avoid doing it again, I try to feel as the student must have felt when I acted inappropriately. By putting myself in his shoes, by remonstrating with myself over my actions, I hope I decrease the chances that I'll repeat this bad behavior. I still might. But I trust that I will do it less, because I will keep the humiliated student's reaction in mind.

Now let's turn to a leader who broke his covenant: a mentor, Paul Nasr, who violated the unspoken pact with his apprentice Rob Parson. This case study resonates with HBS students because they all read it, discuss it, and subsequently never forget it. They don't forget it because they see themselves as characters in the play, as people who have been assessed or treated unfairly. They wanted to have a conversation that mattered and didn't have it or waited too long to engage in this dialogue.

Paul Nasr brings his gifted apprentice over from Credit Suisse to join him in Morgan Stanley's Debt Capital Markets Department. Rob Parson is in the process of transforming the business, moving market share from 2 to 12.2 percent in less than eleven months. Parson is expecting to be promoted at the end of the year, given that he heard in an informal discussion when he joined Morgan Stanley that he would be promoted at year's end if he transformed the business. Parson has done so and more. He has confided in his mentor that in another six months he will take market share to 16 percent. Everyone on Wall Street knows about Parson and the phenomenal job he has done in transforming the business.

The scene gets more complicated because Parson has rough edges in his personality, given his background and perceived slights growing up. He can be verbally abusive, turning from pleasant to screaming in a nanosecond. This weakness runs counter to the type of culture John Mack wants to create within the prestigious financial services firm. If Mack promotes Parson, what signal will that send to everyone else in the firm? Will Mack be speaking out of both sides of his mouth if he signs on to this promotion even if Parson has transformed the business? No one else has been able to do what Parson has done in this area of the business.

But Parson believes Nasr has made him a promise. Eventually Nasr gets around to telling Parson in a very ineffective way that he won't be on the promotion list for managing director given his culturally unacceptable behavior. Parson goes ballistic. He swears at his mentor. He screams at him. He walks out of their meeting brokenhearted knowing that, once again, he has come up short in life. Once again, he built up the courage to trust someone and that person failed him. Parson begins to pull away and through his actions puts the relationship in jeopardy.

As you read this story, you may have decided that Parson was to blame rather than Nasr. But sometimes, covenants are broken in complex ways. While Parson's behaviors may have caused the rupture, Nasr could have handled it differently. Let me give you some deeper context.

Parson has trusted no one as he has Nasr. He doesn't know how to react, so he distances himself. He isolates himself. He focuses on his work but explicitly ignores Nasr. Inside he rages. He works but goes through the motions. For his part, Nasr doesn't want to see Parson because it makes him feel guilty. They act like strangers, and this creates a growing, unspoken tension. The relationship between these two professionals won't ever be repaired. Parson receives myriad offers from other firms. The covenant is broken.

Ten years later, when Parson retires and celebrates by throwing himself a party, Nasr isn't invited. They never reconnected on any meaningful level. You see, when the covenant is broken, it's very difficult to reconnect given the amount of trust that has dissipated between the two parties.

What could Nasr have done differently to maintain the covenant? Nasr could have given Parson feedback early and often. He could have socialized him to the culture of Morgan Stanley. When Parson acted out, Nasr could have processed the behavior rather than pretending nothing was wrong. He could have been more empathic and set a clearer direction. That he didn't says a lot about the difficulty of maintaining covenant relationships. Nasr felt guilty about Parson, and guilt can cause even the best leaders to act in ways that harm relationships.

Sometimes, people break covenants inadvertently. When a student makes an appointment with a professor and the professor doesn't show up, the student may wonder if she isn't that important. If a professor promises to return a paper and doesn't, the student wonders about the relationship. Is the professor really interested in her academic success? Professors sometimes forget to show up and return papers; there is some truth to the stereotype of the absent-minded professor. But the damage to the relationship is the same as if the professor neglected the student on purpose.

The goal is to lead and teach in a way so that students don't begin to slide down the proverbial pole and pull away from the commitment to and with their teachers. It sounds so simple. But teaching and leading through covenantal behavior can be a complex endeavor and requires vigilance—vigilance that's worth it if deep and abiding relationships can be maintained.

Tips and Tactics for Teachers

Earlier in the book I described the preparation needed to teach. Through this process the teacher is setting the groundwork to establish covenantal relationships. Studying the information sheets of the students, knowing their backgrounds, is another obvious example of preparing to create the kind of relationship where the students sit on the edges of their chairs, involved in the process of learning and discovering.

Looking in the eyes of students, listening to them intently when interacting with them, joking where appropriate, calling a student who has had an accident, inviting students for group interactions in one's home, expecting individual office visits, and seeking ways to understand each student are all ways to create covenantal relationships. The list is endless. Stand by the door in the classroom and welcome students as they enter the classroom, and call students by name. Show genuine interest as students speak in class. Walk up close to them as they speak. Send an email to a student who has excelled in class or who is struggling. Initiate communication when concerned with the progress or disposition of a student. Act quickly if you feel you are losing a student.

I want more than anything else to create relationships in the classroom where students are willing to suspend self-doubt and self-consciousness to jump into the learning endeavor. It is those moments of truth that students remember. It is those moments that give students the courage to be different and make real change. I long for those moments. To experience them is reason enough to teach. Nothing in this world feels better.

In comparison, there is nothing more discouraging to observe and experience than a student who communicates a deep sense of disinterest and lack of commitment to self, to others, and to me. One student raised his hand and remarked that he just didn't think the class was grounded in research. He communicated cynicism and distrust of the process. He communicated that he didn't want to be bothered with the content of the course. Needless to say, I took the slight personally and agonized far too long about how I had failed the student. As you'll recall, this is one of my anxiety-based patterns rearing its head. In the throes of my agonizing, I assume the covenant has been broken.

Can I be an effective teacher and not seek covenantal relationships with students? No, I don't think it is possible. That is why humans continue to teach and will never be displaced by computers. While computers can dispense knowledge, it is the process of transferring experience that makes the difference. Clearly, very smart teachers can dispense information as well. But if the human commitment is doubted by the students, then the teacher is simply creating barriers that make the teaching experience more difficult.

While it is natural for humans to sabotage their own efforts through faulty thinking or behavior that is inconsistent with who that person is, why make teaching more difficult? It's hard enough, challenging enough without creating self imposed barriers. At the end of the day, I don't believe it is possible to make the teaching experience transformational with a contractual mindset. If we reflect on our public school systems, many struggling and underfunded, we see professionals who have lost heart, who show up to work believing they are second-class citizens. They walk into the school already on their heels, trying to show students they are in control. We see the result of these daily interactions play out in myriad ways in every part of our lives. Simply stated, "Mailing it in" while teaching makes teachers no more effective than robots.

SIX

The Rationale

What I Teach and When I Teach It

Why do I teach what I do in a particular session? What do I need to consider in creating a curriculum design within a semester? How do I play to my strengths and teach content, question the students' assumptions, and help them learn something about themselves?

As you have learned, I believe awareness of behavioral patterns benefits teachers. Similarly, I want students to understand the patterns that are serving them in productive ways. I also want them to figure out ways to disrupt the patterns that are inhibiting their learning and classroom performance.

I increase the probability of their learning new skills, gaining new insights, and absorbing new content when I possess a sound theory or rationale for what I'm teaching. I also try to be clear about the needs of the students and where they are developmentally. What are each student's development requirements? Given that they are all in different stages psychologically and emotionally during a given class, I must design the curriculum and the eighty minutes of class in a way that takes these stages into consideration.

I wrestle with creating the process that leverages what needs to be taught, how it should be taught, and what the sequencing should be to take advantage of our time together.

Now let's focus on a specific course and a specific class. While I need to tailor my teaching to individual student needs, I also must communicate specific content, content that can be challenging both for the students to grasp and for the teacher to convey. I'm going to start by describing this course and my content goals and then take you into the classroom so you can see how I attempt to implement my lesson plan and the obstacles to doing so effectively.

We'll focus on an Authentic Leadership course to illustrate the methodology behind the madness. The following are the fundamental assumptions behind why I teach this session:

- Leaders must understand the linkages between important conversations and being authentic.

- An investment must be made. Conversations that matter demand something of leaders, so leaders must invest in the interaction to achieve the desired outcome.

- There is a natural gap between what we think and feel and how we assess others based on what we see and hear. Most individuals don't have the skills to reduce that gap.

- Difficult conversations require "deactivation"—settling down with our best intentions as we share what we think and feel in a constructive way.

- Tough conversations require us to be courageous because we don't know what the outcome will be of the conversation on multiple levels.

My goal is to give students tools so they will take care of business relative to tough conversations. With the tools, they will (ideally) become more courageous and thoughtful about the timing and the rationale behind their challenging conversations. Whether they plan on repairing a broken relationship or initiating a tough discussion in the future, these tools will help them.

I also emphasize that the session may feel a bit like a workshop, and it is meant to be. Practical skills are needed to step over the threshold of discomfort into the zone of problem solving.

Successful conversations are not defined by having both parties smile and hug at the end. We cannot judge the outcome based on whether someone likes us at the end of the conversation. Instead, we need to learn how to deactivate ourselves, to give our best selves a shot at sharing how we think and feel constructively. As we share, we must recognize that our conversational partner has the right to react however he or she chooses. Finally, I emphasize to students what difficult conversations are usually about: assumptions, values, interests, perceptions, experiences, and judgments (and predictions about the future).

My Difficult Conversations

Given that preamble, let me share the concerns that run through my head when I'm facing tough discussions, both with students and with other people in my professional and personal lives.

How do I tell my partner what frustrates me about her behavior when she comes home from work? Why can't I tell her what I'm thinking and feeling? Why do I delay having tough conversations with students who I believe aren't doing good work or aren't committed? When I see a student using her iPhone in class, why do I perseverate about how to confront her without ruining our relationship? How do I share my strong opinions to a colleague with whom I'm writing a paper when his effort falls below my expectations?

How do I tell my department head that she needs to deal with another faculty member who is bullying other junior faculty members? How do I speak to students who I believe are taking shortcuts in their preparation for class? How do I tell my daughter I think she is selecting a job that isn't a good fit?

The aforementioned examples are just the beginning of a string of important conversations that I should have, that seem to stare back at me through any given day. Students probably have similar questions and worries coursing through their brains. To understand what these conversations are and how I attempt to teach them the art of tough talks, let's focus on one specific eighty-minute session that falls halfway through the course on authentic leadership.

Introduction to Session

The students have been assigned to read a book on having difficult conversations. More important, they come to class with a difficult conversation in mind that they know they should have or want to have.

Some students will focus on personal issues. They will want to know how to end a relationship or how to communicate their strong feelings to prospective romantic partners. A student may want to know how to tell his parents that he is gay and wants to "come out" to them in a way that doesn't cause distance in their relationship.

Other students focus on previous jobs that they left in part because they were unable to have difficult conversations. One student opined that he applied to business school because he hated his boss and work situation and applying to school was a reasonable way to rationalize the decision and save face—and avoid expressing his feelings to his boss. Another confessed that at her previous job, she fired someone because she was threatened by this individual's expertise. She wanted to rewrite the script, having a discussion with this person she fired so she could come clean about her mistake.

Most of my students have already been considering the topic, contemplating a particular situation that needs attention or repair. In theory and practice, the session on difficult conversations has already begun the moment they have revisited and reflected upon a prior event or situation. So they come to class primed for an intense experience.

On the blackboard I write the following two questions:

1. *If you didn't have the conversation, why not?*
2. *And if you did, why did you?*

These two questions set up an exercise I do later in the session. But I want to prepare the students for the multiple exercises we do in class during the session. I want them to "turn and talk" throughout the session so they can hear their own voices say and feel and taste words that are tough to say—or words they have felt internally but haven't vocalized.

The Class in Session

When the class begins, I have the following situations ready for discussion, ones that involved the need for a difficult conversation. This process is consistent with my philosophical approach of beginning class with a metaphor or story. My style is to give students a visceral experience to capture their collective interest and focus on the topic at hand. I want to get them in the room and engaged in the topic as soon as I can.

I read out loud situations where I had to have an uncomfortable conversation. "During a two-week period last February, the following incidents occurred:

- The snow removal guy shoved the snow so hard against our fence that it shattered.

- Vineeta expressed her frustration that I began to clear the dinner table before she was finished eating.

- My daughter Catharine informed me she had no plans to visit Boston during the summer for the third summer in a row.

- When I arrived in Salt Lake City I went to pick up a rental car, but the company had just rented its last car. They weren't sure what I should do as I stood in the Salt Lake City airport.

- My brother called the day after his birthday to remind me that I forgot to call him on his birthday again.

- I needed to talk with Bill about something he said during the faculty meeting that was over the line.

- A student wrote and told me I had offended him in class by making fun of him.

- A student was overly aggressive in class in response to another student, causing minutes of real tension in the class. I needed to call and talk with him."

Why do I go through this list? I want to make the point that tough, uncomfortable conversations are the rule, not the exception. They are awkward and yet ever present, waiting for us to delay having them, ignore them, or hope they go away. I want to highlight that when students become managers, their days will be full of uncomfortable, gray-zone issues—they will feel uneasy, as will others. And they will need to lean into the discomfort.

Ten minutes into the class, I've given them heartfelt examples of how difficult conversations show up in all of our lives. I've normalized difficult conversations, allowing students to reflect on the situations where tough conversations have been part of their lives. I've also shared the rationale behind why these interactions are not easy but are imperative for dynamic relationships.

I walk through assumptions behind the session. I mention the three key assumptions noted previously but don't dwell on them. Students are often apprehensive because they aren't good at having this kind of conversation; many young adults are carrying around unfinished business as it relates to relationships. Anticipating this, I want them to jump in rather than think too much and become even more apprehensive.

Warm-Up Exercise: Unfinished Business (7–10 Minutes)

I ask the students to think of a time they needed to have a conversation that mattered but didn't have it. Why didn't they have it? What was the outcome?

Then I give them another assignment: Think of a time you did have a tough conversation. Did you get the outcome you wanted? If not, why not? If you did, why do you think you did?

I might also ask them to think of "unfinished business" they have in both their personal and professional lives. Each student selects a situation in each of the categories. If time permits, I might have the students talk to someone in class about these issues. I want them to verbalize, to hear their own voices addressing these important issues.

For example, Devika turns to Jaya and relates the story of a current roommate, Kavita, who doesn't clean up after herself. Devika describes how the situation has evolved and how she hasn't been able to confront Kavita for fear that conflict would ensue, making the situation worse.

One student talked about how at a previous job, he was a manager and had a crush on a subordinate. He explained that he didn't know what to do about it because of the boss–direct report relationship. So he pretended his feelings didn't exist. He didn't want to walk near the woman's desk. He began to flush whenever he passed her in the hallway.

He confessed that he became even more frustrated when this subordinate began dating someone he knew. This knowledge made the situation worse. As the student related the story to the class, students sat straight and silent, completely focused on the speaker—they could all relate to the difficulty he had experienced. The storyteller began to speak more slowly, lowering his voice as he fought back the emotion behind what he was describing. This experience helped the class reach a deeper level of mature vulnerability where it was okay to access emotions, not knowing what the outcome might be.

The Teaching Plan (15–20 Minutes)

Students need to understand the motives behind their behaviors, and whether to have a difficult conversation underscores this subject's importance. This is a crucial task, in that once students grasp their motives, they are better able to deactivate the situations. I ask the students to assess the costs and benefits of having one of these conversations.

Through the processing of the previous questions, we induct three basic reasons to avoid a tough conversation:

- To answer the question, is the real conflict inside me?

- To answer the question, is there a better way to address the situation than talking about it like changing my behavior, just acting differently?

- To answer the question, do I have the wrong goals in mind— change the person, hurt the person, tell the person off?

Some reasons to have the conversation can be discovered by asking the following questions: Am I genuinely interested in learning the other person's story? Do I really want to share my views in a spirit of listening and understanding? Do I really want to problem-solve together?

Here I emphasize one of the themes of the course and session: Don't slide or resign yourself into patterns of behavior that don't serve you. Decide whether you want to have a particular conversation. Act with intentionality.

Too often, we opt for avoidance, which usually makes a bad situation worse. Let me share the story of Jeffrey, a professor who didn't respect or like Jordan. Their offices were next to each other, and at first, this proximity was merely awkward. Over time, though, Jordan found Jeffrey's dislike off-putting, in large part because Jeffrey was a full professor who carried a lot of weight in the department. Jordan wanted to talk to Jeffrey about the reasons for his animosity—Jordan assumed a lot of it had to do with Jordan's well-received publications in a journal that had rejected Jeffrey's submissions—but Jordan could never muster the courage to have this conversation. Finally, the tension between them grew so intense that Jordan resigned and sought a position elsewhere. Not only did the department lose a valuable young member, but everyone except Jeffrey liked and respected Jordan and missed him when he left.

The same thing happens in personal relationships. I know many couples where one member of the dyad isn't happy but doesn't know how to deal with the situation. So instead of talking about the tough issues with the partner, the one member of the couple decides to resign himself or herself to the situation and endure in hopes of not upsetting their children. The secret is that the children already know there is tension and discontent in the marriage. Avoidance of difficult conversations does no good to the children or the two people in the relationship.

Todd and Scott (20 Minutes)

Now let's return to the classroom and a more formal exercise involving difficult conversations. We have a practice run that requires students to analyze a Harvard Business School (HBS) case titled Crucial Conversations (see appendix B). The students receive a form (see appendix A) that asks them to evaluate an interaction between a boss and a subordinate. The case describes a situation where Todd (the subordinate) feels his boss (Scott) has been dishonest with him. Todd decides to act out in counterproductive ways that causes a tense situation.

The HBS students must follow a structured process that follows the theory discussed in *Difficult Conversations*. The students try to understand context that analyzes the story along three dimensions: What happened from the subordinate's point of view, what was the impact and intent of the conversation, and in what ways did the individual contribute to the situation?

The students complete the form, responding first from the point of view of Todd (the subordinate). They do the same for Scott. I try to force students to see another person's point of view from these three different dimensions. I ask students to complete the matrix based on what the other person might be thinking and feeling. What is the reality of the other person? What did the students contribute, what were their intentions, and what was the subsequent impact on them?

I then ask students to assess the feelings behind their attributions and judgments from both perspectives. Finally, we turn to the following question: How does what has happened threaten both individuals' identities? What is at stake for both parties?

I give two single-sheet handouts per person, one to deconstruct the Todd-Scott situation and later to do the same with their particular conversation. I have students get into groups of three and complete the sheet in detail. They process what they have learned by seeing the situation from both individuals' perspectives.

Note: This practice round with Todd and Scott prepares students to deconstruct their own respective conversation they have identified earlier in the session.

Student Practice and Role Play (20 Minutes)

I give the students time in class to complete the second handout regarding their own situation on which they've chosen to focus. Also, I ask students to write the first paragraph of how they will begin the conversation in real life.

The students pair up, and one student plays the role of the person who will receive the message from the student. They role-play the situation and then switch places and do it again. We process as a class what emerged from the role plays.

Session Summary (5 Minutes)

First: I make it clear to the class that I'm not insisting that they have the conversation. I am insisting that they make a choice rather than just resigning themselves to a given situation or backing into a state of being. "Decide, don't slide" is the takeaway.

Second: Some students who have taken this class in the past have spent their time talking themselves out of having the conversation. I communicate that I hope that they have the opposite effect on one another. I want them to express support for and faith in one another.

Third: I highlight the theme of the Internal Revenue Service: Pay now or pay later with interest and penalties. Human interactions, miscommunications, and misunderstandings don't vanish into thin air. They are circular in nature. They will come back in some form until people learn the lesson they need to learn or until they learn the skills of having conversations that matter all the time.

Fourth: This is also an appropriate time to introduce the term *experiential avoidance*: the process of delaying conversations and allowing the tension to build up because of the unfinished business between the parties.

The Moral to the Session on Difficult Conversations

Courage. That is what I want to teach students throughout the course and specifically during this session. Courage is defined by doing something difficult or frightening where you don't know what the outcome might be. I want students to recognize the value of ceding control and trying different behavioral patterns.

Having important though difficult conversations is a daily opportunity to be courageous and discerning simultaneously. I don't believe in confrontation for confrontation's sake; I have no interest in having students walking around delivering bombs to others just to see the emotional effects of the explosion. I do expect students to be self-aware enough to know when to confront and when to be quiet. I expect them be conscious about how and when having a tough conversation will benefit both parties rather than resigning themselves to avoiding tough talks at all costs—including the cost of their quality of life.

Following the eighty-minute class period, the students head off to meet in small groups. I encourage each group to discuss what the group members are planning to do or not do in terms of having an important conversation. I warn them to be aware whether they are colluding in talking each other out of having these conversations. I ask them to follow up with one another through the week to see if they did what they agreed to do.

The biggest challenge in teaching this session is remaining deactivated emotionally so that I don't lose my courage. I want to be teacher, confidant, cheerleader, and fan. I want students to figure out their respective talents and patterns—especially the patterns that are causing reticence and fear. Because we have been together for half the semester, the students trust one another and me enough to explore new ways of considering future career alternatives. The challenge for me is to not sound too optimistic to the students who are feeling frightened and fearful of the future. I have succeeded if some students act and work through their fears. I've never heard someone say that he or she was sorry about taking the step to have an important conversation.

Teaching a class that is equally challenging for students, I want to do everything possible to help them meet this challenge. To that end, I use the "doctor model": See one, do one, teach one. First, I have them observe two people having a tough conversation. Second, I have students engage in a difficult conversation. Third, I give them the assignment of teaching someone outside of the classroom how to have a tough conversation.

I also introduce students to the concept of *affective labeling*, the process of noticing and acknowledging internal dialogue, to help them grapple with the tough conversation challenge. By recognizing this interior voice that may raise all sorts of fears and objections to tough conversations, students can quiet this voice. I've seen how people use affective labeling to calm themselves. During class throughout the semester, we practice affective labeling. Most students become much more aware of what's going on inside of them and are much better able to engage in tough conversations because of this knowledge.

For instance, one student decided to ask her sister why she felt distant from her. I will call her Sarah. She wanted to understand her younger sister and was concerned that the distance between them grew as they got older. As Sarah shared her feelings with her sister during a phone conversation, her sister's silence became palpable. The silence was broken as Sarah heard the sniffles and tears of her sister. The sibling stated that she was frightened to tell anyone in the family that she had a girlfriend, that she was a lesbian. As soon as Sarah heard those words, she began to cry. But the tears were based on relief. They were tears of relief that there was a way to close the distance in their relationship. Sarah stated her support and love for her sister. They cried together. The following weekend they met in New York and her little sister brought along her partner. Over time, Sarah coached her little sister on how to talk to their parents.

Not everyone engages in a conversation like Sarah did. But even those who do will need to understand the danger of not practicing this behavior regularly. By the end of the session, I hope the students are prepared to reflect on how the conversations they are not having have begun to define how they are living their lives. The "difficult conversation" session also sets up the subsequent sessions in which I ask students to interview family members. This session also is a precursor to another session we have on building a support network, how to ask for help, and how to express gratitude.

The end goal is to give students the courage to live more authentically. I want them to experience the process of living more honestly with themselves and worry less about image management. By the end of this session, students will feel that anything is possible and also that life is more challenging when they live from their essence because they must listen more honestly to self. While the short-term discomfort can be powerful, the long-term payoffs begin to show sooner than students expect.

In the coming chapter, I will walk you through what I'm thinking and working through mentally after teaching a class session. I will share with you the postmortem of the eighty-minute session.

SEVEN

The Teaching Session Concludes

The After-Action Review

Teachers improve not only by being conscious of what's taking place in their classrooms in real time but by reflecting on what took place. It's a question of sifting the gold from the stream of consciousness. To that end, I'm going to share my stream of thoughts after I leave the classroom. As you'll see, it's a crowded stream.

After Class

As the period ends, I begin to feel good about the overall ebb and flow of the class session. Collectively, we made progress in the learning process, but why do I feel good about it? What's the evidence that it was a good class, other than that it's over?

In the session, I highlighted the difference between espoused values and enacted values. I had students list the values an anthropologist would observe after watching the students for a year in one column. How do the students actually behave? In a second column, the students listed the values they believe are most important in living their respective lives. I then asked them to see where the variance is between what they espouse and how they live.

How do I do know the students experienced the power of this exercise? What did they make of the assignment to find the discrepancy between actions and words? They have forty-eight hours to act. Are they frightened? Are they rolling their eyes? Do they think the assignment is too elementary? I look for signs of discontent as the students pick up their papers. If there was discontent, what would that look like? I'm wondering whether my search for signs of dissatisfaction is just a product of my anxieties. The class period has been over for a minute and my mind chatter has run wild.

And I go back to the key questions: Did the students learn the content I wanted them to learn? Did I push them in the right ways so they questioned their assumptions about living a principled life? Did they learn something new about themselves? Or am I being naïve and failing to realize that the students are probably not interested in their reflections but are figuring out where they will be having lunch and with whom, or they are thinking about whether they have enough time to work out at the gym or take a nap before their next class or make a phone call to a former colleague at their previous work site?

Am I still just living off postclass adrenaline? There are times that I feel like my mind chatter gains velocity once the class has concluded. I feel scattered, disorganized, out of sorts. Am I breathing? Do I realize that the board cleaners, three students, and the next teacher are all waiting in the wings along with two sets of parents who have been sitting in on the class? Momentum . . . I need to get moving and not feel overwhelmed by the chaos that surrounds me.

As I begin to look at my notes, I realize that students are gathering around me to ask questions or mention their absence in the following class period. Or I am surrounded by ten students standing around the desk trying to ask me questions regarding what transpired in the last eighty minutes. Either way, I am just trying to catch my breath. Do I really have the time to answer the questions or respond to whatever is on the minds of my students? Out of the corner of my eye, I see the next instructor waiting for my classroom. I also notice that the board washers are waiting for some signal as to whether they can erase part or all of the boards.

I also realize that I left my zip drive in the computer and need to retrieve it. I also need to close down the PowerPoint presentation that continues to be projected on the screen and needs to be cleared for the next instructor. As I walk back to the desk, a couple of students are sitting up by the far door next to the sky deck talking quietly.

It looks like one of the students might be crying or close to it. I begin to wonder whether he is reacting to something that transpired in class or whether it has to do to with some extraneous experience. Should I approach the student? Is it any of my business? If the student does want to meet with me in my office, do I have time to talk now? What about my grading class participation? Why do I think I have an obligation to snoop in on the personal lives of the students? I decide to email the student after class so that I don't draw more attention to him. Still, I can't let it go. I begin to imagine the worst; I wonder if it was something I said, some comment I made or didn't make. I ask myself if I should intervene or, at the very least, ask if the student is OK.

I also realize that a couple of students left lunch wrappers in the class. Should I pick them up or hope that the board washers take the initiative and pick them up? Do I mention something in the next class period to the students who may have left them behind? As I leave the room, I see the guests who attended my class, the parents of one of my students. They want to thank me for allowing them to sit in. Their son is standing uncomfortably next to them trying to be inconspicuous. He's trying to talk to friends as well as show faint interest in his parents' conversation with me. But in reality, he probably would rather be somewhere else. As I work myself out of the room to the hallway in the Aldrich building, I feel like I'm exerting an unwanted magnetic pull. Everyone seems to be looking for a nod in the hallway as I pass. Why would I think they want to make eye contact? I typically have one or two students trailing me who want to continue conversation from the class. I question whether they are just sucking up or they really have a question that they sincerely want answered. I try to make the effort to walk and establish eye contact, but my head and heart aren't in it. I really crave some solitude. After the volatility of class, I prefer isolation where I can get myself back on solid ground after the funnel of the tornado has passed.

There's No Place like Home: The Long Walk Back to Safety

As I walk back to my office, I look down and realize that I have chalk all over my pants. I look like a walking blackboard. Did I teach the whole class period with chalk all over me? Does it matter? I wrote on the board at the beginning of the class and haven't touched chalk since then.

I don't remember where I put my zip drive. I have a hole in the corner of my suit pocket. I wonder if it's fallen down in the lining of the suit. Or should I check the computer inside the classroom? No, there is no way I want to retrace my steps. My hope is that someone in Audio/Visual will find it and email me. I wonder how much a zip drive costs.

I remembered that I wanted to pick up a sandwich and a soda on the way back to the office. But how do I purchase food without seeing anyone? I'm for sure not going into Spangler Student Union. I'll just head over to the small café on the first floor of my office building. Hopefully, there won't be a line or many customers. I arrive and buy an egg salad sandwich and a diet Pepsi. I head over to the elevator when I remember

I left my folder with notes and teaching plan sitting on the side counter where Lucia stands near the register.

I also remember that I have a student appointment in twenty minutes. In addition, I need to grade the class's participation. My pace quickens as I see that my wife, Vineeta, is trying to call on my cell phone—I put it in silence mode when I was teaching. Should I pick up? I really don't have the time to talk. But if I pick up, I can at least express my anxiety around time pressure to Vineeta. She knows that my life at work is often managed in fifteen-minute increments.

I decide to pick up. I can tell in two seconds by the tenor of her voice that she needs me to be all in on this conversation. She doesn't want me to fix anything. She needs a listening ear. At what point do I interrupt her and share my real-time dilemma? As she talks, I begin to reflect on whether I will be able to grade class participation after the student appointment and a call I need to make to my book editor. Is it ethical to wait that long? Just how confident am I in my recall of what transpired in the classroom? Typically, I'm overconfident in my ability to evaluate students. It comes with all the road miles I've logged in the classroom. *Arrogance* would be another word for my state of mind. Pure hubris. On some level I know that an MBA won't challenge my grading, or if that student does, he or she will complain to another student and not to me directly. Am I OK with that?

I know that I will need to call Vineeta back right before the department faculty meeting. Do I dare wait until I get home tonight to continue the conversation? Fat chance! The kids will be on me. We will need to pick up the conversation later that night when we are both exhausted with little to nothing in the emotional gas tank. The student who wants to meet with me is waiting outside my office. He announces that he is fifteen minutes early. I haven't had time to use the bathroom, close my eyes for five minutes, and just breathe. I've been going full tilt since 5:00 a.m. When will I get a break to release all the anxiety inside of me?

When I open my office door, the student enters. He begins by telling me how much he is enjoying the class and mentions that he knew very little about psychology until he signed up for the course. I'm impatient; when will he get to the point? He finally explains the reason for his visit: He and his fiancée will be getting married during finals week. He's asked his other professors if he can miss the last class of the semester and explains they're all fine with it. The implication is that I should be fine with it too. I am irritated. I have little to no patience at the moment, least of all for a student who insinuates that missing the class is a "done deal." Or perhaps that is just the way I'm reading the situation. I am irked that he would make this request. I'm put out at my colleagues who rolled over and seem to accept that missing class is no big deal. I feel like this student is going to get the worst side of me.

I become very quiet. Then I tell him I'm conflicted about the situation and that I'm feeling pressure to make a decision that is running counter to what I would typically do. I mention that I need to attend a faculty meeting but that I'll call him that night after I can think more about it and obtain perspective on his request. I'm pleased that I didn't get sarcastic and cynical with him. I wonder whether there is any way for me to like him again. Just writing this makes me disappointed in my harsh reaction to what other professors must have considered an easily grantable request.

Questioning Myself: Learning from the Experience

As I walk to the faculty meeting, I begin to ask myself the usual questions that jump into my head after this type of encounter. I reflect on why I was so unwilling to give the student what he asked for, why I was so hostile toward him. By midway through my walk, my questions segue from this incident to ones pertaining to the just-completed class. These questions stay with me until late in the evening, and most address a single concern: "How did I do?" Related questions that pass through my mind are the following:

- Did the students learn anything today?

- Did I cover what I wanted to cover the way I wanted it to be covered?

- What were the two or three key lessons I wanted the students to leave the class with?

- Did they think class was a total waste?

- Why did some students seem distracted during the class? Was it the content, was it me, or was it the activities they were involved in last night outside of class?

- How did today's class relate to yesterday's class?

- What about the student who was emotional after class? Should I call him?

- When I marked down participation earlier today, I noticed that I focused too much on one side of the class. Is that a common pattern?

- We are ten sessions into the course and there are a few students who still haven't raised their hands. Is it time to send them an email suggesting that they need to begin involving themselves more in the learning experience?

I also realize that I wasn't as excited about the whole session today as I usually am. What is that about? Why did it feel so much like work? Was I working harder than the students? As I reflect on the class, I realize that I looked at the clock more than I typically do. Why wasn't I lost in the classroom experience? Was it the case selection? Why didn't I ever feel like I jumped in the deep end and really modeled how I want the students to be involved? Am I being too critical of myself? Perhaps I don't have a good read on what really happened. After all, two students wrote and reported how much they liked the class. Yet I know both of these students want to get high grades in the course. Are they just manipulating me?

At the end of the day, do I feel like I'm sufficiently uncertain about what took place that I need to talk with another faculty member to gain clarity? I know my patterns well enough to recognize that I typically focus on my limitations, how I messed up the class period, about what I think could be improved. To counter this pattern, I note five specific things that went well and write them down so I have a tangible reminder. This exercise helps stop the mind-numbing process of perseverating about past experiences.

Earlier in the day, after grading participation, I recorded what my insights were from the class. I realized that I spent more time than usual on the first discussion section of the teaching plan setting up the case situation and discussing the context. I gleaned that I was more excited about that piece of the curriculum than any other. The story about Rick being asked by his father, Lester, to take over the business continues to be compelling to me, so I felt I communicated Rick's situation to the class with intensity. This snippet from my notes is an example of capturing what went well. To stop the mind chatter from increasing, I identify what went well either right after class or that evening.

The challenge is to try to separate what I've created in my mind and what actually happened during the day's class period. "Know my patterns" is my refrain. Do I typically find myself falling short in my own mind? I notice immediately when this obsessive self-examination begins, and I simply observe it. The more I notice my patterns, the more I will be able to stop the mind chatter that exhausts me over time.

Before I leave work, I may want to chat for five minutes with a colleague about what went right or discuss the patterns that I have observed. I've had other faculty observe me and focus on a particular area in which I want to improve. As a result, I'm often acutely aware of where I fall short, even though I have improved in these areas because of the feedback I've received.

I focus on what I might do the next day in class. What three behaviors do I want to change or focus on? This focus is designed to quiet the obsession on the past. It will make me feel like I have some control rather than like a victim of the situation, that I'm helpless or simply reacting to students. It will change my mindset from having a tentative stance to having one of possibility. Finally, I do some activity that is removed from my academic pursuits. Read a trashy novel. Read or share an article or novel with my partner. The key is to do something that breaks my typical patterns.

Finally, I sit on the side of my bed and write three things for which I am grateful that day. I record how grateful I am for certain faculty members who make me better and support me each and every day. I express gratitude for the day's perfect weather and that I walked home from work. I note that my child's caregiver loves my child as much as I do. I read my list three times.

I get in the habit of doing this behavior every night. As a result, there will be a greater chance that the following day I begin to look for the positive things in my life. I will begin to reframe my way of seeing the world. I will begin to train my mind to focus less on simply surviving and more on different pedagogical methods.

Once the two student appointments are over, I can pay close attention to the grading even though it was a couple of hours since the class finished. I've reviewed where my blind spots are and what I might do next time to address the issues. I realize that I still have confidence that I got the grading right. How would I check that assumption? Arrogance is again paid for in no small measure by the students.

I'm going to ask my closest friend of forty years and colleague, Paul, to sit in on the next class and get a sense of whether he thinks I'm really connecting with the students. Do they seem to be committed to the process? Do they listen and participate in thoughtful ways? Do I seem interested and engaged or does it seem like I'm going through the motions? In the meantime, I will reach out to Willis Emmons, director of the Christensen Center on Teaching and Learning. I'm going to have him review some of my materials and past teaching evaluations.

I've recorded previous sessions, and I'll ask Willis to review the tapes with me so that we can slow down the teaching process frame by frame. The hunger for feedback continues. Why? I know I can teach. But am I improving? I could almost fake it. That should worry me. Willis will help me come to grips with whether I'm playing not to lose. In the coming chapter, I will discuss the evaluation process, my reactions to them, and my sessions with Willis Emmons, the faculty shaman on teaching and learning.

Josh Coval teaches here at HBS in the finance department. He is a good teacher. He loves his research more. He loves his wife, Leslie, also a professor at HBS in organizational behavior, and his kids even more. But he's always trying new adventures. He and Leslie took sabbaticals for a year and went to China with their children. They traveled throughout Australia. Their kids are young. I wonder whether Josh will continue teaching here. Why? One day in passing he told me that his mantra is "Life begins on the edge of our comfort zones." Do I even know where my comfort zones are? Am I just too comfortable with teaching? What would a stretch look like for me?

Asking colleagues and friends for feedback is a scary necessity. I still become frightened when I ask people to watch me teach and tell me where my blind spots might be. I'm still surprised when they point them out, but I'm also relieved that I've become aware of these issues. Invariably, they spotlight an aspect of one of my patterns.

As long as I maintain awareness of my core patterns, I won't teach by rote; my patterns keep me on my toes and stop me from going through the teaching motions mindlessly. My pattern of seeing my efforts as either failures or successes and nothing in between is still nerve wracking, but it's who I am. Having basic questions about my abilities will always be a part of the journey. It does keep me on the edge of the cliff. It is exciting to a certain extent. But what I hope is that it keeps me improving step by step without taking me over the edge into the abyss.

EIGHT

Reflections from a Room with a View

The Meta-Conversation

At the end of the day I find myself sitting and staring out of my office window with a view overlooking both the tennis courts and Peterson Park. Because of this great view, my office is often considered the best office at Harvard Business School (HBS).

After-Action Review Continues at the End of the Day

The moment I gaze out of my office window at the end of the day, I find myself calming down and decompressing. My heartbeat has returned to a normal rhythm. I see a few of my students passing by and heading off to catch the bus or to work out. I see a group of twenty petrified-looking, prospective students gazing straight ahead, each dressed to impress, following a guide.

One of my goals for the students is to have them stand back and face their own life path. An underlying assumption is that the students will do less harm if they are aware of why they do what they do. They will hurt themselves and others less if they understand the purpose and path they are on. I don't pretend that they should have an answer, but I would like them to be asking questions about their journey before, during, and after the experience at HBS. It's ironic that the course on authentic leadership begins with how we appreciate and get over, around, or through our past. As I look out my third-floor window at the students and staff playing tennis, I realize that my life's journey is intertwined with their time at HBS. I'm thinking about how teaching the course informs my own thought processes and how I relate to the past.

The Past

My patterns are deep and intertwined. My narratives inform how I live today, how I taught today. I accept the fact that I will always be driven to accomplish tasks. My ability to laugh at myself is healthier today than years ago, and I can also laugh at my struggle for self-acceptance.

It occurs to me that for a long while, it was difficult to admit these patterns existed. It was easier to take refuge in denial. I suspect most teachers possess similar reactions to their patterns. But to become more effective in the classroom, teachers need at least a modicum of reflection. Without it, they won't be aware of their patterns and won't be able to change for the better. Over the years, I've observed a lot of teachers, and the ones who resist introspection never learn, never grow, and never become more effective.

Now let's return to how this introspection works in my classroom and in my head. The first three sessions of the course introduce the notion of personal stories or narratives that guide how we think and feel and behave. We also focus on how we lose our way along the journey. What are the signs we are getting close to the edge? How do we self-regulate in real time? How will our ongoing fears play havoc with our ability to take prudent risks?

Contemplating these observations, I realize they are based on my distorted view of my past. Though I recall what I've experienced, I often distort reality. I remember spending two years creating a collection of nickels. I'm also convinced that my older brothers took the collection and went to our local corner market and spent my collection on candy. At a family reunion this past winter, my younger brother got angry at our older brother for blaming my younger brother for stealing his collection of coins. How can this be? Between you and me, I know with 100 percent certainty that my story and not theirs is accurate. This is me making a joke; as I noted, I can laugh about these things now.

I do believe I live now based on a distorted past where I may have compressed experiences or even combined certain memories from two different events. But to me they are real. As I re-create the stories of my past, I realize that my siblings, for example, are convinced they have memories like elephants. Each of us has a different picture and narrative about our family and the way we saw the family interact. But regardless of their accuracy, my memories inform how I see my current situation. I thought our family was tight knit and highly engaged with one another. As I grew older I realized that I was highly engaged with my parents, but my other four siblings were not. We each describe family dynamics from our own vantage points. I'm the only child of the five that would describe my relationship as warm and connected. I'm the outlier.

I know I'm not alone when it comes to these perceptions. I'm not the only one who has gone through a crucible, and I'm not the only one who is affected by those long-ago experiences and bears the scars still. As a large group of students walk by, I note to myself that teaching the students every year about confronting and overcoming crucibles is balm for my soul as well. When does the class begin and end? I'm not sure it ever does. That is why the past connects and influences how we live in the present.

Do I have the ability to keep a clear head as I observe students creating their own narratives? Do I have perspective on my shortcomings, my crucibles? How do I define failures and reframe them to be viewed as opportunities to learn? Students have told me about ongoing abuse in their families. Some have discussed current relationships that frighten them. Some have lost parents at an early age. For others, the hardships have been more subtle; they are brilliant students who have never felt accepted by parents for who they are, only for their outstanding academic achievements. The list is endless.

As I gaze out the window and reflect, I question whether I'm helping students become more adaptive. Will they make it through their next crucible with greater resilience? Can they maintain a clear head in times of crises? Do they become paralyzed with fear? Do they wait for someone else to save the day? Are they unable to be the people they were before they experienced the hardship? I want them to be able to keep tough feedback in perspective. I want them to be able to be direct when a tough conversation is necessary.

The Present

How do the inside and outside relate to one another? Do I have the ability to explore my own self-awareness along with the students? Appreciating what is happening simultaneously inside of me and externally in the classroom is one central goal. Have I been able to push the students to question their rationale for doing what they are doing? Do they have a theory of how they experience other people? Do they have a sense of how others experience them? Most important, do they know what happens inside others when they are in a group? These questions are fundamental to the whole idea of leadership and what it means to empower others.

I obsess over whether students are becoming more self-aware; this awareness is crucial if they are going to make a difference in the world. To earn the trust of others, they must be comfortable in their own skin and conscious of what resides beneath the surface. If they're not self-aware, other people won't take them seriously; they will seem superficial, lacking the depth that comes with self-examination.

Are they aware whether they live the values they espouse? Do they know the difference between their espoused and enacted values in everyday life? What are their responses when they begin to cross their own lines of self-regulation? Do they know what their boundaries are? Do others know what their values are?

Self-awareness of motivation is another core issue. Have my students considered their intrinsic and extrinsic motivators? How much does the task at hand drive them? Do they love what they are doing? Have they found their sweet spots that intersect the three circles of capabilities, others' perceptions of their gifts, and their true passions? Have they assessed feelings of being trapped, of lacking the freedom to change their career course? Do they see their options as making cliff decisions or wedge decisions?

Cliff decisions emerge when we believe that the only answers to the issues we face are dramatic changes. I would be making a cliff decision if I felt the only choice was to leave the university because there was a colleague I didn't trust. These are decisions that may be an overreaction to a situation that could be solved with less dramatic outcomes. If I made a wedge decision about remaining at the university, on the other hand, I might ask to move out of the department or I might sit down and have a conversation with my colleague in order to smooth out the situation. Even if I decide to teach with another colleague rather than the one I distrust, I've made a minor change and have not overreacted.

Here are some other questions about which I ruminate. Do the students relate to the concept of career anchors and how their values, motives, and needs combine to create career drives? Career theory would suggest that we need to have myriad experiences before we can home in on a better career choice. We need to have "road miles" so that we, through the process of elimination, understand the intersection between our values, motivations, and needs. Why are the students anxious to find the "right career" based on their motivations without having many road miles traveled in their lives?

Do the students understand the power of communicating horizontally as well as vertically? Do they talk with others or to others? Are they enhancing their current relationships based on how they interact? How much of the interaction is self-focused as opposed to being genuine interest in the other person? How much time and effort are spent trying to understand the realities of others? Listening becomes a lost art. Are the students are too obsessed with achieving their own tasks, crossing more and more items off their lists? I obsess about whether students possess the courage to have authentic conversations that connect with others. I hope they realize that mature vulnerability brings meaning in their daily lives.

Every session in the course includes a pause for participants to look for and appreciate blind spots. The students need to push learning where they are frightened to explore. What parts of their lives are blocked from the view of others? There is a time and a place where the sharing of new information brings greater self-discovery. What are the appropriate ways to have students share in a safe environment where they don't later regret their openness? As we seek to understand those areas of ourselves, we come to grips with our ability to have compassion for others—and more important, compassion for self.

Typically when I look out the window of my office, I find myself focused more on appreciation and gratitude. Today I'm making connections between the three sections of the course. While the past and present are essential, the ultimate goal is creating a future that has meaning and gives students opportunities to develop themselves and others.

The Future

Research on individual change proves the power of integrating support into the change process. I have received such support throughout my life. We ask students to report on a time when they needed help but didn't ask for it. We follow up by asking them to relate a time when someone else came to them for help. What was the experience like? Were they capable of creating a network that served them just as they supported others?

Part of the support emerges from our personal relationships, an existing network that might include spouses, friends, and siblings. Yet we often devote ourselves to tasks at work and allow personal relationships to suffer from neglect. Am I emphasizing this enough to the students? Are they even aware that most relationships at home are focused on getting through life rather than developing more meaningful and enduring relationships? I try to highlight that we need not only to focus on the integration of work and play, of home and work but to be more aware of the quality of the life we create with those who are near and dear to us.

As I reflect on the future, I realize that I have set up the class to integrate layers of experience, content, and self-reflection so that students are able to create a purpose for their lives. That is the ultimate goal for students to achieve. With the assistance of their learning groups, they create a statement that serves as an iron rod of sorts, a center pole for living their lives. As the students work with and give feedback to one another, they create a guide distilled from their course experiences.

This guide is related to purpose. For instance, one student may discover that she is guided by a commitment to making the world a safer place. Another student may learn that he wants to help others live more congruent lives. In class, I share with students purpose statements that were created by other students over the last few years. These are statements of intent, of focus, of hope for the future.

Once they've found their guide, they have created the conditions to examine and reflect on how they can empower others. Have they come to grips with their desire to lead others? Perhaps through the class the students realize they don't want to be out in front.

Perhaps the students believe that they don't have the capabilities and passion to empower others. A few feel guilty because they want to make a difference in the world, yet we've given them few options beyond running a company. Hopefully, through their adventure in studying authenticity, they have built up enough courage to follow the right path for them. I strive to create the conditions where students leave the course with the confidence and intention to live life on the edge of their comfort zones.

The central theme of the course is to create the space for students to focus less on image making and more on living from their essence. They must know how to communicate and relate to themselves in nondestructive ways and learn to listen and focus on others and what others need. We hope to remove the barriers that the students create for themselves that hinder their growth. The desired outcome is to help students understand that they judge others based on what they see and hear and assess themselves based on how they think and feel.

We've been conditioned to behave in ways that conform, to hide behind our fears and to take the road most traveled. I am trying to free students to explore different roads. Most important, I hope to imbue them with enough courage to explore new ideas and experiences, even if the unfamiliarity makes them uncomfortable. I hope that the students learn how to "self-watch" in real time in order to activate or deactivate how they are thinking, acting, and feeling.

NINE

Life Away from the Pit—Musings on University Life

Connections and Disconnections

The fabric of the school is created by the staff, faculty, and administration. It's created in the interactions among a diverse cast of characters that includes nonacademic personnel like the landscapers and custodians. The cumulative effect of so many interactions among individual actors is a spirit, a feeling, an atmosphere that permeates an institution. Just as students leave classrooms and focus on those activities that are more central to their lives, faculty members find themselves in the web of institutional relationships.

The individual-versus-collective dynamic is often evident in universities. Outside the classroom, faculty members are supposed to interact, fostering a collective spirit. Those attracted to university life, however, are in the main individual contributors. They are a type of entrepreneur, creating their own startups based on their research, their interests. Mixing with others can feel like an unnatural act to many professors. They have a penchant for maximum autonomy, individual work as opposed to team play. They want to be included but don't want to take on administrative work that might take them away from what makes their hearts beat fast. The technical and functional work is what defines them. They maintain positive self-concepts only when they continually produce enough and cross enough activities off their lists. Their credo is "Who I am is solely based on what I accomplish."

The glue of the school is created in the hallways of the faculty office buildings. Each department has its own norms in terms of whether faculty members are supposed to work from their school offices. In most departments, you can walk the halls and hear the latest gossip. What you won't hear in the business school hallways is a discussion of leadership theory or an organizational behavior concept. The topics fluctuate between who is not working hard enough in the department, who has or has not published recently, who is preparing for the promotion process, or the inadequacies of department and school leadership.

If we find ourselves chatting in subsequent days, the conversation meanders back to the regular topics. While we occasionally focus on a colleague's teaching ability or research accomplishments, I've observed that we end up spotlighting where colleagues are coming up short. Different faculty members rotate as the objects of the conversation, but the themes remain basically the same. I don't know whether we need to blow off steam by talking about others or whether we just gossip as a way of connecting on some level with our colleagues.

On occasion we can be raucous. If I'm sitting in my office and I hear loud laughter outside the door, I wonder what I've missed. In more insecure moments I wonder if I'm ever the topic of conversation among the faculty. Somehow I think I'm above the fray.

I do know that if we are talking about Bill and Bill turns a corner and is heading our way, we change the topic in a nanosecond and create the illusion that we were chatting about some other topic. We have the ability to include Bill into the conversation and evolve into gossiping about someone else. Bill becomes part of the conversational circle rather than its target. It's quite remarkable how deft we are at real-time conversation, creating the impression that we are authentic in word and deed.

Within this milieu, creating strong, reciprocal relationships can be a challenge. So how do we create connections in a world where individuality is the norm? University leaders grapple constantly with this question. They strive to create an atmosphere where those who primarily work alone want to be at school, chatting in the hallways with their colleagues and students. Adding to the challenge, faculty members often believe that their time away from campus—on research trips, in their home offices working on papers and books, at forums on their academic topics—is where the real creative work takes place. Nonetheless, deans and department heads continue their search for answers around inclusivity and connection.

Validation

One of the easiest ways to connect with others is through validation. Validation involves acknowledgment and affirmation. I'm not suggesting giving others insincere compliments to stroke their egos. But validation does have everything to do with noticing when colleagues, staff, and students do good work and acknowledging it. Validation also means paying attention to and being interested in something other than one's own agenda. Validating someone else is communicating that you are "aware." You are committed to focusing on what the other person might want to accomplish. It is the process of trying to understand the reality of someone else.

It costs little to express gratitude outside the classroom, but it can reward both parties with a sense of connection. Last year I ran into a fellow teacher, Julio, who unlike me, never took himself too seriously. He was kind and tough simultaneously in the classroom. He never cold-called students, yet invited them to participate. He pushed and prodded students to think deeply in real time and not simply say something. If someone was struggling in his classes, he coached the student offline. Julio came to my office twelve years ago to thank me for guiding him when he was section chair of one of the ten first-year sections or communities. He didn't make a big production out of it; he just walked into my office and said, "Thank you." He continued, "I have been scared to death to have this role and you have reached out to me to see if I needed anything."

I bumped into Julio at the dining room in Baker Library years later and noticed how gaunt he appeared; I told him he didn't look well. He said, "I thought most everyone knew that I have a rare form of cancer." His response stopped me in my tracks. I replied that I didn't know what to say; I did thank him for telling me.

After lunch I returned to my office, suspecting that my lunch guest may have noticed that I was there but not really there. My heart and mind were still wrapping themselves around what Julio had told me. On my walk back to the office, I ran into a younger professor I'll call Joanna. Joanna was denied promotion. Her research was seen as good but not great. Her teaching was off the charts. She could hold students spellbound with her intensity, her understanding of the content, her unparalleled energy. I watched her teach twice, and both experiences were memorable.

The encounter with Joanna will always be linked with my earlier encounter with Julio. The unfairness of life struck me. Why was Julio the one to get a horrible disease? And why was a great teacher denied a promotion? But my thoughts were even more focused. It made me question the origins of teaching ability. I asked myself how a junior faculty member could learn the art and science of teaching with so little experience in the classroom. I wondered if I really believed that teaching was something that could be learned or whether it was an innate gift. Joanna taught me otherwise.

And most relevant of all, reflecting on Julio and Joanna made me realize anew the need to reach out to colleagues and to students. Unless we make a conscious effort to reach out to these individuals, they may be gone before we know it, and all we're left with is regret. By forging connections, we create a sense of inclusiveness that benefits everyone and makes us feel like we're part of something larger than ourselves.

Paying for the Sins of Others

Joanna was denied a promotion largely because two senior faculty members didn't like each other. Their callous disregard for one another spilled over in the decision-making process of hiring, developing, and evaluating other faculty members. It seemed obvious that Joanna would be promoted. Yet these two professors had very different opinions about Joanna. One loved her work, her approach to research, and her teaching abilities. The other faculty member took the opposite point of view. In fact, these two members of the department took the opposite point of view on virtually every departmental decision.

Though the vast majority of department professors believed Joanna should be promoted, she paid the price of unfinished business between two faculty members. She paid for the sins of senior faculty who refused to consider Joanna's promotion on its merits. They both became more dug into their positions the closer they came to having to make a decision. Their warfare was a result of the disconnectedness that one often finds in academia, and it harms both faculty and students.

But let's examine Joanna's story in more detail, since it reveals the petty politics that can prevent the best teachers from being promoted and lower department morale.

Joanna was a new professor with big dreams and ambitious plans for her career. She arrived at Harvard Business School with streams of glory following her. Family members and graduate student friends celebrated her appointment for days. Teaching in the required curriculum, Joanna hadn't taught MBA students before. Joanna and the students had some trepidation, given all they had heard from alumni and friends about the Harvard MBA experience. Joanna needed to observe and get a feel for the students, guiding them on their educational journey for her specific content expertise.

Joanna knew she would be supported in a teaching group consisting of anywhere from five to eight faculty, all assigned to teach the basic curriculum of a foundation course. Each MBA in the first year will be taught the same material. Joanna worried that she wouldn't hold her own in the classroom compared with the other new teachers and seasoned faculty. What happens if she embarrasses herself in the first few sessions of the course? What happens if some student challenges her, points out an error in her computation, tries to "one-up" her in front of the class?

On the first day of class, Joanna feels comfortable being in front of the ninety-two students, though she has a typical case of nerves initially. Still, she feels in command of the room. As the class unfolds, her confidence continues to increase. After the class, she reports back to her teaching group that she thinks it went well. The chatter in the hallways among students is that this new faculty member is awesome in the classroom. The semester ends. The evaluations come back for Joanna. She is rated a 6.3 on a 7-point scale. The teaching group is supportive. The course head sidles up to Joanna and tells her he couldn't be more proud of her.

Each year Joanna's scores improve until after four years at the school she is ranked as the best teacher in her group. After four short years, she has a reputation as being one of the best teachers in the school. But alas, for some reason, one of the senior faculty members resents her

fame. She resents that Joanna is complimented on her teaching whenever the two colleagues are together. Joanna begins to hear whispered
innuendo that her research is questionable. No one is explicit about the
problem, but Joanna begins to feel a bit paranoid.

Joanna decides to be proactive and ask senior faculty members what
she should do to enhance her research and her standing in the department. Most senior colleagues give her contradictory advice. She begins
to feel more anxiety when at school. After a while, Joanna starts isolat-
ing herself. Rather than interacting with established faculty members,
she gravitates toward younger faculty members whom she met four
years earlier in socialization activities. Invitations to teach in executive
courses diminish. The department head pulls Joanna into his office and
tells her that she should withdraw her promotion packet.

Joanna leaves the school seven months later, in June, to accept a tenured position at a competing school. But Joanna really didn't leave in
June. Her heart and soul moved on in late November when she was told
she wouldn't be promoted. Older faculty visit her and tell her they can't
believe that she was denied a promotion. Everyone acts aghast. But no
one steps up to accept responsibility for the outcome.

The senior faculty member who felt threatened by Joanna for some
reason can't make it to the 2:00 p.m. farewell gathering in Joanna's honor.
At the gathering, Joanna is presented with a book that highlights the
history of Harvard University that will serve as a reminder that she came
up short. She's told it's perfect for display on a coffee table. That way
every visitor can be reminded she didn't succeed in her first efforts as
a professor.

And to the victors go the spoils. Two or three more young PhDs
are hired for the upcoming fall. The process is repeated each year by
every department. And we wonder why more faculty members don't
get through the system and become tenured faculty. I'm biased, of
course. I'm not talking about just Harvard but about most universities. Businesses suffer from similar problems. Institutions organized

around partnerships especially suffer from promotion processes that are poorly defined and often misunderstood. "Joannas" exist everywhere, in academia and business.

The irony of the Joanna story is that she was doing well until hints were dropped that she hadn't impressed everyone. And everyone needed to be on board for her to make the next step up the tenure-track ladder. In typical fashion, younger professionals paid the price for questionable management and mentoring. We could blame the department head. We could blame all the senior faculty members. We could blame a flawed promotion system. We could blame the dean for not re-creating a system into something more meritorious. We could blame Joanna for not demanding to be managed.

Organizations sell alignment as the solution to this problem. Yet alignment breaks down when younger people are penalized for poor leadership. Over time, the spirit of the place turns more to cynicism than to commitment. I know that my friend Joanna left for a great job. I miss her. I wish we had been in the same department. I'm not sure I could have helped along the way. But I do know that achieving connection and commitment makes work exciting. It is soul work. Sometimes that connective work is strategic and sometimes just intuitive, real-time action or behavior that focuses on reaching within and between two colleagues.

With hindsight, I wish I could have helped Joanna the way I've tried to help students who are struggling. I don't always succeed, but the effort to create connection and commitment seems to be a crucial part of a professor's job.

The Reward of Connecting with Students: Nate Bihlmaier

May 20, 2012: I received a phone call in London, where I had just landed to teach at a law firm. Nitin Nohria, dean of Harvard Business School, was on the line. He asked me to come home immediately, explaining that an MBA student was missing. Nate Bihlmaier was a student to whom I was close. We had discussed careers, marriage, being a parent, being a leader of an organization. I had met him two years earlier on the first day of his MBA studies. I was his section chair (adviser for ninety students), his instructor for the first-year Organizational Behavior course, and he visited me often throughout his two years at HBS.

Nate possessed a wide smile, a wry sense of humor, and a giving heart. He was confident and humble at the same time. He was one of the few students from the state of Kansas who was getting his Harvard MBA, and he never let anyone forget it. No matter what the topic of the discussion was, he would work Oswald, Kansas into the conversation. His fellow section mates pretended to be bothered—not another Oswald, Kansas reference—but we found Nate endearing.

Five days before his graduation from Harvard Business School, he headed for Portland, Maine, with two section mates to celebrate their fast-approaching graduation. We later learned that he and his buddies went to a bar, but Nate stayed there after his friends departed. On the way back to the hotel, he lost his footing and fell into the harbor next to the bar. His body was found three days later, forty-eight hours before he was to walk across the stage to receive his diploma. Instead of Nate attending his graduation, he was represented by his wife, his brother, and his father. Together they walked across the stage to receive his diploma from Dean Nohria. The dean hugged all three in the middle of the stage in front of thousands of attendees.

Five days later I flew to Wichita, Kansas, rented a car there, and drove four hours northwest to Oswald. I had gone to Nate's home to attend a memorial service at the community center and represent the Business School. I was asked to speak during the service. I sat for late lunch on picnic tables with butcher paper covering the tables under the roof of the old center. It was a barbeque of sorts. Everyone from miles around showed up in their Sunday best on a very hot Friday afternoon; the temperature was nearly ninety degrees. All of us were sweating through our clothes and no one cared. The memorial service evolved into something akin to a Quaker meeting, with those moved by the spirit to share their witness of Nate. The service lasted nearly four hours. It felt like thirty minutes.

One month after my visit to Kansas, I was asked to visit the dean's office. I was given a letter from the dean that was found by Nate's wife, Nancy, as she cleaned out Nate's car to sell. He wrote it two days before he went missing that night in Portland. The letter had fallen down between the seats. He had meant to send it to me. Here is what he wrote:

What are the expectations of a faculty member to reach out to students? Typically, an ebb and flow of communication exists with each student in the class. What I've found most satisfying are the conversationally brave moments with students, catalyzed by their expression of one concern initially when in reality they want to talk about something else—something more personal or difficult or complex. I do know that I will never be the same after experiencing the loss of a student. The way he lost his life adds to the sadness. I miss him.

The connection I had with Nate and have with other students energizes me. It is what returns me to the classroom year after year. It is the same reason I attend graduation each year, so that I can meet parents and connect the generational dots. In the spring of 2017 Nate's cohort returned to HBS for its fifth-year reunion. I already found myself perseverating about how to acknowledge Nate's passing in a way that wouldn't detract from the spirit of the reunion. The mentoring of students in the context of learning how to lead and live is a central reward of my professional experience.

TEN

700 Sundays
Keeping Perspective

What happens if you throw a party and nobody shows? What happens if you plan a second-year elective course and no one shows? After forty-five years of teaching, why does the thought enter my mind at the beginning of every semester? Why would I fear that no one will show up for my classes? They always have and will continue to do so. At least that is what forty years of experience would suggest.

Why 700 Sundays? Ten years ago, my wife and I went to the old opera house in Boston to see Billy Crystal in a one-act play tell his life story. Crystal titled the show *700 Sundays*. That was the number of Sundays he had with his father before his father passed away when Crystal was fifteen years old. Through acting and old photos, Crystal shared with the audience his youthful experiences in Long Island and his observations watching his father as a musician. Billie Holiday and other artists would sit around their living room and play their instruments and sing. Crystal would draw attention to himself by mimicking the musicians and telling little kid jokes. The evening at the theater was mesmerizing.

However, I will never forget how we ended up in the first row right in front of the stage. We had bought less expensive seats. We were sitting in the back row of the theater, close to the lighting and stage managers. Three minutes before the show was to begin, an usher asked us if we would be interested in moving up to the first row. Some decisions are easier to make than others. We quickly got up and followed the usher down the theater aisle. Right before we sat down, the usher told us, "Mr. Crystal wants every seat filled in the first ten rows of the theater so that he doesn't fret about attendance, about whether or not the theater is full. He can only see up to the first ten rows. That's where he focuses. He can see the faces of the audience. So he doesn't want any empty seats."

Could it be that someone as famous as Crystal, someone who has emceed the Academy Awards seven times, still has mind chatter that revolves around whether he "has it"? How can that be? Isn't Billy Crystal more secure than that? How much positive reinforcement does he need to feel good about himself? I began to reflect on whether he too lives with an either/or mentality. At some point, you would assume that he has to understand that he has made it big in his field.

Perhaps my anxieties about whether I can measure up to the best teachers have to do with defining who I am by the external feedback I receive—it's something a lot of professionals do. Perhaps Robert Kegan of Harvard School of Education had it right when he underscored that a stage of adult development called the "interpersonal stage" is defined by how many individuals we convince each day how competent we are. That is how success gets defined. And it's a dangerous game to play. It's a game that by and large can't be won long term.

Rather than Billy Crystal being focused on the one thousand people in the audience that night or that his show had five sold-out dates in Boston, he apparently was worried about his own mind chatter during the show when he saw two empty seats. We know that humans have an easier time focusing on negative experiences than on positive ones.

Negative emotions can be accessed faster and experienced more acutely. Plan a celebratory dinner and arrive to find out you will be seated forty-five minutes late. Head to the restroom to find it dirty. Be seated next to a kitchen door. Months later as you recall this experience, you realize that even though the food met your expectations, you can only remember those unexpected moments.

Kegan suggests that if we use external criteria to define success or happiness, we will come up short, given the powerful influence of our negative-remembering reflex. Perhaps Crystal remembers that one night in Boston when there were two empty seats for his performance. Everything gets distilled and reduced to one reflection or observation. The technical term for this cognitive process is *asymmetric effect with a negative bias*. It holds us captive in everyday life.

Junot Díaz and the Cambridge Public Library

Junot Díaz won the Pulitzer Prize for Fiction for his novel *The Brief Wondrous Life of Oscar Wao*. He was honored for his ability to write about the common man in uncommon situations. He also claimed a Mac-Arthur Genius Award in 2015. He speaks to standing-room-only crowds frequently. He holds an audience captive. His use of tone, pacing, and body language make attendees at his talks never want to leave. In his writing courses at MIT, the small group of students are at once enraptured, intimidated, and praying they don't meet faculty expectations—by what they say in class and more important, what they write for it. They hold their collective breaths as he returns their papers after grading. While Díaz dresses unassumingly, his countenance is riveting. He wears his expertise and status well.

Two years ago, my wife was invited to hear Díaz speak to the city workers of Cambridge in the auditorium of the public library. Five minutes before he was to begin speaking, there were no more than fifteen individuals in the audience. When the designated hour struck, there may have been twenty-five people in an auditorium that could hold three hundred.

I was one member of the audience. I was tracking the speaker out of the corner of my eye trying not to stare. I wanted to see how he was going to adapt not only the presentation to the relatively small audience but how his attitude and the tone of his talk would be affected. Would he be angry that his time had been wasted? Would he talk down to us? Would we as an audience be worthy of his efforts and ask questions that were worthy of him?

At five past noon Díaz was introduced by one of the Cambridge Library librarians. The introduction was short and to the point. The author had basically an hour to fill. I realized that Díaz had begun his connection with the audience before the allotted time began. I noticed that he introduced himself to a number of the attendess. He asked them questions about where they were from, what their work was, and what they liked reading. By the time he was in front of the group, he had already begun to make a connection.

Díaz pulled out his iPhone and began reading from his most current book. He read for five minutes. He then asked the audience why they thought this meant so much to him. Why did he choose to read this passage at this moment? The discussion felt more like friends chatting in a living room. It was warm and intimate and very conversational. I realized that being able to adapt to a particular space and time was key to what Díaz was doing at that very moment and also what I tried to do intuitively.

Inner and Outer Space

I obsess about having the right size of room for whatever audience I'm addressing. I am like Crystal in that I want every seat taken. I always call the registrar well before the first day of class and ask the number of students and the number of seats in the classroom. If I'm teaching a seminar, the table and number of chairs at the table are important. Each place at the table should feel special. All eighty-two students who take the course on leadership need to feel like the course was in demand. It needs to feel intimate. The same holds true for larger audiences.

The larger the audience, the more intimate the stories need to be. I must focus on the details, describing the shade of the moon, the reflection off the water. Drawing the audience in is the key. I might even speak more quietly so that students need to lean in to hear me. I see the fort I would build in the den of my house on Stephens Street in Southeast Portland. I remember how safe and secure I felt being in the fort that might barely contain three eight-year-olds. But I felt safe. I felt like I was protected from the outside world. That is the feeling I want to project inside a classroom, where I can invite students into a lab focused on understanding the human dimension in great detail. No doubt, space is important to many teachers, but it is especially crucial to my teaching style and goals.

The Tug of War between Reality and the Narrative

I want to create allies in the classroom. I want to convince students that I'm not going to waste their time. I will create an internal ally—or at least make the attempt—who essentially is my internal voice. This is what I hear in my head as I teach, the voice that narrates my performance in real time. I'm trying to manage this voice, figure out the appropriate content and process to communicate with the students, and determine what they are thinking, not only about themselves but about what they think I'm thinking while I'm teaching.

My interaction with one student is a metaphor of sorts, illustrating the danger of jumping to conclusions about classroom events. Rather than assuming that Matt is an insensitive, arrogant overachiever, only caring about himself, I reframe my perception—what I think he is doing and feeling when he is walking out of my class. What makes me think that everything that happens in the classroom relates to me as the center of the universe? Once I converse with myself and chat with my inner voice, I realize that the possibilities are endless in terms of what might be going on with all the other students, with Matt and with me.

ELEVEN

Why Managing, Mentoring, and Teaching Overlap

Leaders Take Notice

Mentoring may seem like one task too many, given the current academic environment. We know that expectations for faculty have increased dramatically over the last twenty-five years. Every few years, faculty members, for example, are asked to add more administrative assignments to their already full plates. There are more cross-school activities. There are an increasing number of faculty meetings and faculty symposia where younger faculty members feel pressure to appear and participate as a litmus test for commitment to the institution. The competition to publish in the best journals has increased. Even though fewer professionals read the articles than in the past, publication constitutes a metric that is quantifiable. It is clean and antiseptic and straightforward. It is also an increasingly important criterion in promotion decisions. Faculty members often feel underappreciated and overworked regardless of how much work they actually do. Output is less relevant than appearing overworked. We pride ourselves on our feats of teaching endurance where we have taught a number of consecutive-day sessions. Like football players after a game, we return to our offices wearing evidence of our effort with pride—covered in chalk dust.

Working with a younger faculty member or spending time with students, on the other hand, lacks this same heroic thrill. Thus, the environment is not conducive to taking on the added responsibility of mentoring. In addition, senior faculty members may not be eager to mentor people who seem to possess different values and goals than they do. It's not unusual to hear a senior professor complain that the younger faculty members were raised as Millennials or Generation Yers, meaning that they want everything now and have little to no patience.

In fact, this is a poor excuse not to mentor, especially because it's generally myth rather than reality. What younger faculty members want more than anything else is to be reassured that there are senior faculty members who care about them, care about them deeply.

I often ask senior executives who are in their late fifties or sixties to write down the name of a mentor they had at some point in their careers, who cared more about them than about his or her own career. I tell them that if they think about it, a picture of this individual will come to mind, and you'll recall this mentor almost demanded that you succeed. This person was there when you hit rough patches and was there to give you immediate feedback in real time. The mentor represented you in promotion and compensation decisions. Most important, you had a different experience of yourself because of how that person managed you. You felt like you could accomplish anything.

When I ask young professionals, be they academics or managers, to write down the name of a mentor who fits the above description, they look at me as if I'm speaking another language. They can't conceive of an experience where a more senior professional would take such an interest in them. Nonetheless, younger professionals want what their mentors wanted. Unfortunately, many of them aren't getting it because of the demands placed on the manager/mentors. Teaching, giving feedback, and spending time with subordinates continue to be the first things to fall into the "nice but not essential" category. In business, manager/mentors are more focused on hitting numbers. In academia, they are more focused on publications and classroom demands.

Senior people give up too fast when it comes to mentoring. At the end of the day, the young academics and professionals only want what their bosses received earlier in their careers. I hear senior faculty members and senior professionals wax nostalgically about the good old days when subordinates didn't need to be coddled. But in fact, their memories have faded; they don't remember how they grew and learned and developed. Veteran professors tend to slough off their mentoring duties in the same ways that senior executives do; the latter outsource their teaching or counseling roles to external coaches. In the academic world, that may mean not prioritizing reaching out to younger faculty members. Or it may mean assuming younger faculty will be mentored.

The worry that I have for organizations as well as universities is that strong ties are being created with no one or with the wrong professionals. In every university and company, an individual exists who is best able to mentor younger faculty members and direct reports. Whether it's a professor or a manager, this individual is in an ideal position to mentor because of the emotional intimacy that builds as a result of the relationship over time. Yet for various reasons, many veteran professors fail to take on a mentorship role. The time commitment is what creates the biggest barrier. Time and attention to a younger faculty member doesn't show up on the metric sheets, on the documents that are shipped to the dean's office for the dean's perusal. This can add to their star power as an intellectual or lead to competing offers from other universities.

One of the ways senior faculty members deal with their own guilt about not taking on this role is by making broad-brush generalities about millennials or Generation Xers. They snipe about how new workers don't want to work hard. Or that they need constant feedback. In fact, these younger generations want just the same thing as older generations wanted and received. If I believe, as a senior faculty member, that the younger generation is lazy because of how the younger generation was raised, I can blame the younger generation's parents rather than myself for failing to mentor.

I've seen time and time again where the mentoring has been lax and senior faculty members have decided that someone shouldn't be advanced. Not only do these older professors fail to mentor, but they come close to shunning the younger faculty member. They avoid contact with the younger teacher. I've seen deans intervene and move younger faculty members to other departments when this avoidance occurs; in most instances, these younger faculty members flourish in different environments.

What's discouraging about this situation is that too often once we decide someone won't succeed, we behave in ways that sabotage younger professors, consciously or not. We don't show up at seminars they're leading. We may visit their classrooms yet never meet after the class to share feedback. We don't establish less formal ways to communicate, such as meals or coffee. When younger professionals ask for some feedback on a paper, we don't follow through and give them our insights.

Soon junior faculty members become discouraged, begin to isolate themselves, and ruminate excessively about their careers. They begin to spend more and more time alone in their offices. Senior faculty members hope that the younger professionals see the "writing on the wall" and decide to send their résumés to other universities. At the next Academy of Management meetings, the younger faculty members will spend most of their time networking and seeking faculty positions at other schools.

What Makes a Mentor

Chase Peterson, then president of the University of Utah, gave me the confidence to rise above my inner doubts. Chase and I met when he wanted to discuss my views on organizational change. He supported me in setting and seeking stretch goals. There was never a situation where I didn't feel secure enough to try something new. John Mack, former president and CEO of Morgan Stanley, confronted me when he thought I wasn't happy in my position at the financial services firm. He told me that looking gloomy wouldn't help my efforts in transforming the talent management system at Morgan Stanley.

John finally told me that I should consider going back into academia if I felt I would be more aligned there with my talents. Whenever I was with Peterson or Mack, I wanted to be better. I didn't want to let them down or disappoint. It was as if they were older brothers. I dedicated my last book to them. Chase has passed away. John is thriving after having left Morgan Stanley. There isn't a week that goes by that I don't think of one or the other. They aren't far away. When you experience someone like Chase or John, you will be changed forever.

Chase was never in a hurry. He would ask me questions about how my semester was going and wanted to know the latest research on change management. Once or twice, he even requested my advice on how to handle delicate personnel issues.

One evening I attended a dinner party at the home of Chase and Grethe, his wife. A few students reporting on their global travels for the school would be there. He also invited senior members of the administration as well as the former president of the university David Gardner. As soon as I walked in the door, I realized that I was underdressed. All the men had suits or sport coats or ties on. I wore a V-neck sweater.

Before I could enter the main dining room to meet everyone, Chase went upstairs and put on a V-neck sweater. I could see what he was doing immediately. Nothing was ever mentioned that evening. The next day I called him and pointed out what I had observed the night before. He downplayed the event, but I was touched by his compassion, by his mentoring humanity that extended beyond the school.

John Mack took me under his wing on a number of occasions. In the first month at Morgan Stanley, after we had moved to the East Coast, John and Christy Mack (along with the company's chairman, Richard Fisher, and his wife Emily) hosted an elegant dinner at the Blindbrook Country Club in Westchester County. Joe Perella, Richard Kauffman, Bill Reid, and I were being honored for our decisions to join Morgan Stanley at a senior level. John made sure that I was sitting next to the chairman at the head table. Since I was the nonbanker of the bunch, John wanted to send the message that I was not to be messed with. It wasn't just that John made this gesture; it was that he made it skillfully and in a way that demonstrated his caring as a mentor.

Over the years, I've tried to emulate what I saw in the day-to-day actions of these two great, mentoring leaders.

And so, the questions I ask myself are: Will students want to be better leaders because of their interactions with me as one of their teachers? Will they in turn be the mentor for many others through the years?

Office Visits

Student visits to the office are integral to mentoring, yet these visits give me pause because, depending on my state of mind, I question motives. Why are they really here? Have they been told by counselors that they are close to flunking out so they need to visit each teacher? Do they have a real issue? And what is a real issue relative to a superficial query? Why am I questioning them at all and not taking them at face value?

To make the most of the thirty minutes available for the conference, I begin every meeting with the same question: "How are you doing?" I then listen. I look at the students intently and experience the silence if there is silence. I don't try to fill up the space with just chatter unless I sense that students simply want chatter. But if I feel that's their motivation, I ask them, "So it feels as if you'd like us to get to know one another?" But I try to get to the deeper reason for the meeting if there is one so that we can figure out what a successful meeting would look like at the end of our time together. By setting this goal up front, I'm much more likely to mentor effectively and address this goal in our conference.

I may not get to the second question if students want to talk about why they are doing well or not so well. However, I usually follow the first question with a simple query: "How can I help?" Most students don't know how I can help other than doing what I'm doing. I'm simply a mirror, reflecting why they are experiencing a challenging situation where they are lost or overwhelmed.

The goal for me is to get students to think of alternatives for dealing with the problem. Most important, I want to adhere to the philosophy of Rollo May when he emphasized that the helping professional's first and foremost goal is to "imagine the realities of others." That is my mantra, and in my experience, it's what makes mentoring work.

What I've realized over the years is that I want to understand students and colleagues and know their realities, and I want to communicate to them that this is my purpose. I want to know their narratives, those stories that inform how they live. This means that in one-on-one meetings I'm listening far more than I'm advising. It means that I'm asking more questions, reframing their responses, not hurrying them. I just want to be fully present.

In office meetings, we both learn about common worries related to class or our outside world, and I learn about students' concerns about what their futures hold. I know that they are in large measure carrying the worries of a myriad of stakeholders—parents, siblings, friends. And they don't want to let anyone down in the process. Inevitably, many of them do let them down in some form or fashion. Expectations of others as well as those they have of themselves are often unrealistic, but given their successes, they feel they can exceed all expectations. Not possible but still a goal.

First-Impression Mentoring

Mentoring can begin at first sight and can last for years. Relatively early in the hiring and socialization process, I begin to intuit whether a new hire has the ability to remain at the school long term. I'm not quite sure why I think I'm so insightful to make judgments about young faculty members. I guess I feel like I'm sort of a seer, gazing into the future and discovering that the new faculty member isn't at the school anymore.

I don't overtly sabotage the new colleague. I do make a decision about how much time and effort I want to expend working with the particular person. I ask myself, "Is it worth my efforts? Why don't I work with someone who I know will make it through the system?" Only when I type these words do I realize the irony of my thinking process. Perhaps the fact that I explicitly or implicitly begin to withdraw from the person may play some role in that individual's fate. Perhaps when other faculty members observe that I and some of my colleagues with influence are backing away from a young professor, they jump on the bandwagon and our initial reactions are confirmed—we dismiss someone early on, and that individual is dismissed later.

The same thing happens in business. Too often I see managers in organizations predict when a subordinate will implode. And I get it. In some odd way, the ability to predict the future is gratifying: "I told you he would never work out." I'm assuming that others will recognize my ability to evaluate the quality of human potential. This illusion plays havoc in real economic terms. We hire a new faculty member and spend large amounts of money hiring and moving the scholar to Boston, only to short-circuit the process by pulling psychological and emotional support. Just when the new faculty member needs support.

Instead, I support some other young faculty member who I believe will be successful in all dimensions of academic life. Many of my colleagues do the same thing and withdraw support the fastest from those who are struggling. We may create the illusion that we are helping or interested in their careers, but it is largely a fairly bogus effort. It is what I call deeply shallow conversation. Act intimate and interested but only pretend. Most everyone knows it's a charade. But we've had enough practice to understand just how much eye contact, voice intonation, and spatial distancing are necessary to communicate that you can't be saved but we will be cordial and not shun you.

If you are a star from day one, we all trip over ourselves to include you. We figure out ways to take some credit in the individual's good luck, the positive outcomes. This insight relates to my core pattern of spending too much time in either/or thinking. The colleague is either making it or not. Black and white. Star or goat.

But regardless of patterns, many professors put on an act. We pretend empathy and some regret that it didn't work out. But we quickly move onto another topic like whether we will attend graduation or where we might vacation during the summer. It's comforting to conclude our verbal jam session by ending on a positive note. It feels better all around.

Managing Up: How to Impress

Three years ago, a senior colleague came into my office to ask me a question about one of the junior faculty members. He was worried that the new hire was disingenuous on occasion. John said, "There are times I'm with Mary that I feel like I'm being managed. It's like she tells me exactly what she thinks I want to hear. She has the uncanny ability to know what I'm going to say or want to hear before I say it. I find it off-putting. Every couple of weeks she will find a way to compliment me about how wise I am or how I perform magic in the classroom. It's just not necessary. Tom, at the end of the day we give tenure to those that we want to hang out with, who we can be together with without feeling managed or manipulated. What's your experience of this person?"

John seems taken aback by my reply. I asked him if he would like just a bit of historical feedback related to himself and his perceived style. When he assented, I said, "John, when you were new here I felt the same way about you as you feel now about Mary. But I didn't have the courage to say it then. As I think about my own career journey through academia I think I honed the art of figuring out what I sensed senior faculty wanted to hear. I could smell it. And I responded accordingly. So I was a pro at it. In fact, I don't think you were as good at it as I was. You should have practiced more."

My observation is that everyone manages up to serve his or her needs. Everyone. I don't think people even know they are doing it because it has become so natural. Whether it was learned as an infant and practiced for a lifetime, I have no way of knowing. But I sense that in relatively flat professional service organizations like universities, while the hierarchy has few levels, it is highly political. It matters how the senior faculty see you. It matters what people say about you behind closed doors, in other hallways, in senior faculty meeting discussions.

I remember one assistant professor whom I mentioned early in the book. He couldn't make a comment without referring to three other senior faculty members by whom he had been influenced. Whether we were in a large school faculty meeting with two hundred professors or within the department confines with twenty faculty members, I could predict he would acknowledge someone who had been a big help in mentoring him. It felt so obsequious in word and deed. I asked him to come visit my office at his convenience.

I have great affection for this faculty member, and that helped facilitate our conversation. Fundamentals were in place for me to be direct and share my perception of a particular behavior that I thought wasn't serving him. When I gave him three examples, he tried to explain each one away. I remarked on his defensiveness. He said, "But I don't ever want to be seen as someone who wants all the credit." I replied, "Why do you seem defensive, like you have to defend yourself?" He said, "Because I'm embarrassed. When you point this behavior out, I see it, I see myself doing it, thinking I am being mature, but I'm just trying to impress others by showing how much I know and how many faculty with whom I've worked. I feel like crawling in a hole." I said, "You are already in a hole. How can I help you get out?" He sat quietly. I came over around my desk and began to beat him up in a playful way. I told him that I was the only professor on campus who was perfect. We laughed together.

In the next faculty meeting, he caught himself twice getting ready to list off the names of faculty members with whom he had discussed his research. Each time he looked over at me he saw that I had a wide smile on my face. He managed to say what he wanted to say without referencing anyone, and after the meeting I teased him. We then went our separate ways. My belief in having covenantal relationships—that of mentor and mentee—played itself out in this scene with a positive outcome. The interaction strengthened our relationship.

My junior colleague knew I would not hold back because of the mentoring "rules" we had established in our relationship. At the same time, the relationship is a two-way street, and I urged him to visit and observe my classes so he could give me constructive ideas to enhance my classroom approach. He had very good insights. I was impressed by his insights. I followed through on what he advised me to do and it worked. The relationship became even closer. I felt more commitment to tending the relationship.

TWELVE

Five Warnings

Why This Ride May Be Hazardous to Your Health

Over time I've developed an internal warning system—a system that alerts me to cognitive distortions that continue to emerge in my teaching experience and get in my way of achieving the optimum teaching experience. Warnings are necessary because these distortions visit me at times that I don't expect them. I wish they wouldn't, yet that wish doesn't seem to hold any sway over their existence.

So here, I want to give you fair warning, describing the distortions that visit me and what I do to prevent them from affecting my desired outcome of using every minute in class as a time for learning and developing. I suspect that these five distortions affect many teachers one way or another, so I'm raising a yellow flag that might be advisable for a teacher to heed.

Balance with the Positive to Avoid Focusing on the Negative

I find myself returning to the internal dialogue that reminds me of my negative or self-doubting narrative rather than my self-affirming story. I find that my negative voices are louder than my positive ones, and so I lose confidence and my classroom persona is diminished—I am unwilling to push myself as a teacher, failing to try something new or push boundaries, since these classroom behaviors all carry risks. The technical term of this phenomenon is *asymmetric effect with a negative bias*—a term I introduced in chapter 10. This process highlights why humans naturally focus on negative in a given situation rather than the positive.

Humans anchor on negative emotions more frequently than they do on positive ones. Positive emotions dissipate more quickly than negative emotions. The older we are, the more worried and concerned we are about having negative experiences. Thus, through the aging process, we risk less and learn less and take fewer chances so that we don't have a negative experience.

The goal, then, is to remind ourselves that we possess a positive story, not just a negative one. We need to think about what we've done right as teachers—our strengths, our successes. In this way, we can continue to take risks and stretch ourselves.

Label Your Affect to Avoid Losing Perspective

J. K. Rowling, noted author, has had a major impact on the reading habits of a generation of children. Seldom had there been an author who caught the imaginations of millions of children through books. Obviously, millions of adults also indulged themselves in the world of Harry Potter and friends.

In 2008, Rowling was awarded an honorary doctorate of letters from Harvard University for her written work and her impact on society overall. As Ms. Rowling approached the podium to speak to the audience of well over twenty thousand students and guests, one could observe that she looked nervous. Throughout Harvard Yard there were large screens where guests could view Rowling as she spoke. The camera had the ability to zoom in on the author to see her splotchy skin, with nerves emanating through the skin. You could virtually see her heart beating. She held onto the podium so tightly it looked as though the podium might begin to rock back and forth.

After acknowledging the other dignitaries on stage, she metacommunicated with the audience. Rowling opined, "Ever since I was invited to speak and receive this award I have been apprehensive and somewhat off-center. You see, I am most likely the least educated person here today." As Rowling spoke, you could see a transformation of her countenance right before us. She began to feel calm and grounded. She felt in control of herself and the crowd.

What Rowling had done was label her affect. She had communicated to her audience and to herself that she was right there, in the present. She wasn't focused on the future or the past. In reality, what we know is that fear appears within us as we obsess about the past or the future. Notice that Rowling had initially become obsessed about the future and what her feelings and thoughts would be like when she appeared at Harvard speaking. She had created the feelings and emotions she expected to have at Harvard back when she received the invitation to speak. The process that took place cognitively was what is called "affective forecasting." Humans believe they can predict what they will feel like, what they will look like, and what their experiences will be like. In truth, they are terrible at predicting accurately their emotions and feelings in the future. When they walk into those feelings they project, they seldom get it right. But they continue to forecast their affect.

Rowling had experienced one of the more central behaviors of humans in attempting to predict the future. After those months of worry, she used "affective labeling" to bring herself to the present, where her oration on innovation and creativity entranced the audience.

Embrace Clarity and Simplicity to Avoid Ambiguity

The problem here is the confusion and misperceptions caused through ambiguous behaviors and messages sent by those acting unintentionally. I've written about this outcome before. It is near and dear to my heart. I have caused pain in the process of intending a different outcome. I use my humor to tease and to create endearment. Not everyone experiences it that way.

I remember reading in my teaching evaluations on more than one occasion that a student was frightened to come to class. Each has communicated in different words, but the feeling and meaning seemed the same. One response was representative of the other. "Professor DeLong, when you make fun of someone in class it's hard to trust you. I come to class in fear that you may tease me or make a sarcastic comment about me. I just don't find the classroom a safe place. As these words hit the page, I feel a sudden jolt of embarrassment and some shame."

This is what I know and believe: If we send ambiguous messages or act in ways that are unclear or confusing, the receiver will conclude that something is wrong or that the receiver did something wrong. The receiver will surmise and conclude wrongly that there are distance and doubt about the nature of our relationship.

There have been situations when I was running to one classroom after concluding a previous class experience of teaching. My mind is focused on the next class. I'm focused on getting to class, adjusting the technology, setting up the boards, organizing my teaching notes, buying a bottle of water, meeting a student's parents, taking attendance, and other immediate matters. I am unaware that as I left the previous class a student walked up to me as I was gathering my papers and told me that he had really liked the case we studied that day. I barely acknowledged the comment. I barely even looked up from the table in front of the class. Once I put the papers in the manila folder, I turned quickly and headed for the swinging doors in the Aldrich classroom.

The thought pattern that transpires internally with the student is as follows: "I wonder if Professor DeLong didn't hear me. If he did hear me, he just blew me off! What a jerk! Couldn't he have just acknowledged me? Why was he in such a hurry and not interested in me? I made a comment in today's class and thought it was worthwhile and moved the discussion along. Maybe it wasn't that good after all. But my friend in class told me she really liked it. I thought up to now that there was a chance for me to get a "1" in this class. Maybe I've been fooling myself."

As I step back and analyze this interaction that took all of two seconds, I wonder why I didn't at least say "Thank you." I'm not sure why I behaved as I did. But I did what I did. I wonder how many ambiguous messages I've sent in the past month. Most important: Every student in both classes that day could write a chapter in a book describing a time when he or she communicated an ambiguous message that was interpreted in a way that wasn't the intended meaning of the sender. Each student in the two classes could write another chapter describing a time he or she misinterpreted a message sent by a boss, a parent, a friend. In both chapters there was pain caused that wasn't intended.

I could have simply stated to the student who paid me the compliment, "Thank you. I'm pleased that it resonated with you. I'm sorry I'm so rushed right now, but I have to get to the next class. Let's catch up another time." Given the amount that all of us are attempting to accomplish each day, we are always running faster and faster, often with little understanding of the way our behavior is interpreted by others.

The goal is not to please and live just for others, to meet their needs, to create a smooth and silky life methodology in hopes that we are loved by everyone. But the goal might be to be understood, to communicate in ways where our intentions shine through. The goal could be to deactivate ourselves and put our best selves forward in order to leave a trail of speaking with truth, with support, in a direct manner that is simple and clear.

Assist the students by telling them to find one other person they don't know. Find another student to join their group. Find a third and so on. Each group should find an open space in the classroom where the group can discuss specific questions provided by the instructor in class. Have the questions on a handout or prewritten on the board.

Tell the students that after they have written down their collective answers, they are to select one of the group members to communicate to the rest of the group the three key learnings. Step by step. With clarity and simplicity. This approach will counter the confusion that may arise if students are lost in the instructions. Manage the ambiguity through structure.

Use the Magic of Horizontal Communications to Overcome the Power of Least Interest

Humans want symmetry in relationships. What doesn't work in relationships is when there is asymmetry or perceived asymmetry in a relationship. We want to be talked with, rather than talked to, by another person. We don't want another person to communicate that that person is more important, has more power, and has more control and influence in the relationship.

Naturally, when a student walks into my office, there is asymmetry because of my position or perceived knowledge or the understanding that I will be evaluating the student. The student is coming to my office, so I'm in a secure place that is familiar to me. The student can feel intimidated, less sure of herself, on foreign territory. In the office I have all the symbols of status, such as awards I've hung on the wall or the obvious location of my office in the corner of the building. I also know that when the student enters the room, the student wants something from me. The student wants information, more insights into my thinking, an answer to a question.

My operating principle to deal with the asymmetry in the relationship is to ask three basic questions at some point during the meeting. First, I'm going to ask the student, "How are you?" Second, I'm going to ask what I can do to assist or help the student. Third, I ask the student for feedback on how I might improve my teaching style or how I can enhance the classroom learning environment. The students who respond to the final question by saying "Everything is just fine" don't meet my expectations. I want the students to learn how to give feedback when students are in conversation with those in authority. I want them to learn that they shouldn't silence themselves because of fear of retribution or because they are intimidated.

A piece of the rationale for doing what I do with students during office visits is to teach courage. I want to teach them that they are attending a graduate program that is founded on the importance of general management. The school assumes that students want to manage and inspire others. We also assume that part of communicating is to be honest when communicating in all directions. When I was in the working world of Wall Street, I saw professionals lie to one another and speak ill about others to others. I witnessed subordinates agreeing with their bosses when I knew the subordinates not only didn't like their bosses but didn't believe in what they just agreed to. My hope is that those small interactions in my office give students reps in speaking truth to power.

When students, partners, employees, or children act out, part of the motivation is to test a relationship. One person in the relationship believes he or she has less power in the relationship. The person in a relationship who has less interest in the relationship has the most power.

When we act out, we are trying to discover the nature of the relationship and whether or not there is symmetry in the relationship.

A way to reduce those feelings of insecurity and imbalance is to understand that there is a higher likelihood of keeping balance in the relationship if we talk with rather than to the other person. Talking with another person infers equality. Sharing information rather than telling another person infers respect. Remaining deactivated by empathizing with another, by listening, by being direct quietly rather than acting hostile creates symmetry. The concept of the "power of least interest" is basic and fundamental to our ability to form relationships that are meaningful, that create connection, that create reasons for living and loving. The ability to notice when you are becoming activated, finding yourself talking down to others, using your finger to make a point, yelling at another person, demanding of others rather than requesting—these are all signs that you have moved beyond or beneath the expectations of communicating with rather than to others.

Keep Conversations Small to Cure Experiential Avoidance

Last year I was mentoring an assistant professor on ways to enhance his teaching. After observing a couple of classes, I set up a follow-up meeting with this professor. The meeting was set up for three days from the previous observation. At the last minute, I needed to rearrange my schedule and cancel the feedback session. There was a part of me that was relieved that I could put off the meeting. I had seen some behaviors that had me worried about his ability to manage a classroom.

When I rescheduled to meet in two weeks, I felt immediate relief. I could literally feel the anxiety leave my body. The tension dissipated, and I felt compelled to move to the next agenda item on my "to do" lists. I forgot about the meeting I needed to have for about two hours. But then what I experienced was the tension coming back that I previously had thinking about the meeting I needed to have with my colleague. But the anxiety was more acute. The proverbial "rock in my shoe" felt larger and more annoying.

I called my psychiatrist daughter and told her of this experience. I told her that every time I delayed having a conversation I needed to have, she began to chuckle. She informed me that the phenomenon I just described was in fact a normal response when we delayed having a conversation. She called it "experiential avoidance." She suggested that each time we delay a conversation we know we need to have, the greater the tension. Sara mentioned that in time, if I delayed the conversation endlessly, I would begin to see this heretofore small conversation as a major event. Major events that we have created in our heads and that we feel in our hearts seldom turn out as planned.

One reason these events seldom play out as we think they might relates to the aforementioned cognitive distortion of affective forecasting. Another reason they often go awry is that the more we plan for these events in our heads, the more times we practice how we think the scene will play out. Once we are in the moment of that scene and the scene goes in a different direction, we try to steer it back to the one we planned. The more we have practiced with the end in view, the more we don't want to cede control or at least share responsibility for the conversation.

When we practice experiential avoidance, rather than giving direct and timely feedback, we delay the process of helping to develop the other person by simply putting off the interaction. The longer we delay having the conversation, the higher the probability that we won't ever have the conversation or that it will do harm to the relationship.

Somehow we seem to slip through life avoiding conversations that could cause tension or could be unpredictable. We will fall short as teachers and leaders if we choose to avoid these important opportunities to create clarity.

THIRTEEN

Hungry for Feedback! Oh, Really?

When our oldest daughter was fifteen years old, I decided to show a modicum of courage by asking Sara how she thought I could improve as her dad. Throughout the years, Sara had been reluctant to share her insights. I think part of Sara's approach related to how safe she felt around me. Also, I think she felt a need to take care of me. Her need to please and her silence during contentious conversations in the family taught her that the price might be too high if she disagreed with my point of view.

At some point I did want to know what I needed to do to be better at the art of fathering. I was naïve and frightened enough as a father in my thirties and early forties to assume that I was doing a good job as dad. I knew I could be funny around our daughters. I knew their friends liked to be at our house and that they enjoyed me being around. Of course, the play friends were no older than nine years of age. I played hide-and-seek with the girls, went on walks, and took care of music lessons. They came to me often, particularly when they needed comforting.

As they grew, and I aged, I continued focusing on my strengths as father, not on my developmental needs. I'm not sure what the specific incident was that inspired me to ask Sara about my style as dad. We were riding in the car on the interstate when I blurted out a query about where I needed improvement. I noticed that my heart was beating a bit faster when I asked the question. She responded immediately, without an edge, with enthusiasm. She averred, "Oh Dad, that's easy. When my friends come over to play, could you just come introduce yourself to my friends and then leave? You hang around too long."

The Myth of Seeking Feedback

A colleague admitted that even though he was required to receive evaluations each semester from his MBA students, he never looked at them. He stated, "Perhaps I'm too insecure. But one or two negative comments take their toll on me. It's just not worth it." I realized that I have an approach-avoidance reaction when I know that I can view my evaluations. The irony is that I tell others how important it is to receive honest feedback in all areas of your life. Yet, at the end of the day, I don't know many leaders and teachers who relish the thought of reviewing student evaluations. Students often mention they want feedback on their work, but it feels like the only ones asking are those who know they are doing well. Or the student knows that he or she might be in academic trouble, so the student is panicked about his or her future at the school.

In this chapter I will not only discuss from whom we can receive feedback but also push back and suggest that there is little evidence in the world of business where developmental or evaluative data bring about behavior change. After over thirty-five years in both the academic and business world, I know of only very few cases where professionals attributed evaluation processes or developmental programs as the impetus for change. They do mention mentoring, but that is a different process from written feedback forms. I will also walk the reader through a mentoring experience initiated by me but led by Willis Emmons, the director of the Christensen Teaching and Learning Center at Harvard Business School (HBS). I will explain the process he led through videotaping and studying myriad course evaluations over a period of three years of my work.

Evaluation versus Development

Evaluation presupposes that the information collected will be used in the decision-making process as to whether an individual is exceeding, meeting, or underperforming based on certain criteria outlined by the institution or organization. The challenge in these programs is that the population being evaluated seldom trusts the system. The efficacy of these programs comes under scrutiny because those administering these programs (or the leaders responsible for them) don't articulate how the information being collected will be used. Thus, participants may collude and ensure that no one gets poor ratings. More important, participants make sure they and their friends are on the same page in terms of how to score the items. The data collected in these processes are hardly accurate, highly skewed to the positive. Qualitative data that are collected are full of "corporate speak."

Sarah has made progress this year. She is nearing the norms we have in our department. She is on the right path.

Samir is outstanding. Everything he touches improves. He is a giver both in processes and with people. Inspiring.

Are we really going to make promotion decisions based on this kind of information? Further, while we have lists of criteria and matrices that create boxes for promotion level and criteria for the relevant level, seldom do compensation committees and promotion committees adhere to the criteria when pressure rises in the committee rooms. "Deciders" digress to personal relationships, those we love or hate. We care less about the outcome from an organizational standpoint. Rather we care most about our relationships.

To this point, no one at HBS knows whether or not student evaluations are used in promotion discussions. We believe they are, but we are told at the departmental level that they aren't taken into consideration when promotion discussions arise. Oh, really?

Developmental Processes

Who is responsible for the development of another faculty member? Do we have a systematic program where mentors are assigned (programs like this seldom work)? When I joined the faculty, there were senior faculty who were invested in my development. If at the end of the semester I access my student evaluations, what do I do with them next? Once I read through them, do I make specific, measurable outcomes that I will monitor from semester to semester? Not once in twenty years have I been asked by a department chair how I was using my evaluations to become a better teacher.

What I've learned over time is that as long as I am above a certain score (5.4 on a 1.0–7.0 scale), no one will ask me about my teaching. When I joined HBS, I had already taught for thirteen years in universities. I had road miles in the classroom. I wasn't at the ten thousand hours of practice but was very close. But I realized that when I studied my feedback, when someone said something I felt was negative, I looked for countervailing data so that I could discount the developmental messages. No one except for my friend and colleague Willis Emmons has ever seen my evaluations to my knowledge.

How did I use the data from the evaluations? I looked for consistent themes that jumped off the page from previous years. Use of humor, confusing summaries, and disorganized discussions came up year after year. Below are examples of comments made in both the positive and negative columns.

Competing with Other Faculty

When I began teaching at HBS, I knew fairly quickly that I could hold my own in the class. While I worried excessively about the quality of my teaching, I knew the students were engaged and seemed to be invested in the educational process. Yet I would be disingenuous if I didn't admit that I wanted to be one of the best teachers at the school. Even though my scores would consistently range between 6.5 and 6.9, I held my breath every time I heard they were going to announce the teachers of the year voted on by the students. In twenty years, I've never won the award. It pains me today to admit that it means so much to me. A goal unmet. My competitive nature on full display. Paul Marshall, an old friend and colleague at HBS, won the teaching award three times, once in each of three consecutive decades. I've watched him teach. I've watched videos of him teaching. He is good. But that much more effective than I am?

It's not that I don't value my colleagues. Don't get me wrong. Out of one side of my mouth, I admire them. From the other side of my mouth, I'm muttering to myself, how can the students be so swept up by these other faculty? Anita, Frances, David, Das, Gunnar, Joshua, Srikant, Malcolm, Catherine, Rawi, Luis. These colleagues are all great teachers. I love these colleagues. Only over time have I begun to realize that depending on whom you ask, some faculty members would talk positively about me.

This is where feedback and development are crucial. It would be great to have a proven, effective process to help faculty members assess their skills and provide tools to strengthen areas where they're weak. Without that, all we can do is ask the questions I ask myself: Have I changed that much over the years? Have I made significant improvement over the years in the classroom? Do I believe that a strategic, explicit plan has made the difference, or was I just born with an interest and a desire to teach? If I agree with the previous statement, I have to ask whether I really believe we can train educators to be better in the classroom or whether those colleagues mentioned above were simply born with the gift. I've seen younger faculty develop over time. I've seen them visit with Willis and with other faculty and genuinely improve. But they initiated the intervention in change. That shouldn't discount their efforts or the subsequent outcomes.

But how much better off would we be if we had a proven process in place to help everyone learn, grow, and become more effective at their craft?

Seeking Feedback in All Directions

At the end of the day, I believe that we will live a delusional life if we don't get out of our comfort zones and seek data that will allow us to question whether or not we are getting in our own way because of the beliefs and actions that inform our behavior. The fact that I wrestle with my evaluations and how others experience me is useful to me in that it's valuable to acknowledge data that make me uncomfortable. Learning can mean discomfort. Learning can mean not knowing the outcome of our behavior.

I would be remiss if I didn't highlight other places in which we might get data about our impact on others. While this chapter focuses mainly on the classroom setting, we faculty may want to entertain other ways to find mirrors that reflect back to us how we interact with the world. For example, for years my children have told me that they don't know when I'm being serious or just teasing, being playful. They can't tell by my affect. This message is consistent with student feedback over the thirty-five years of teaching. Why shouldn't these behaviors not show up in other parts of my life? In the classroom, with my children, with my partner, with fellow faculty, with my bosses?

Colleagues

One of the true weaknesses in the tenure system in higher education is that there is the possibility that I might have certain colleagues forever. Forever. As a result, we're reluctant to level with people whom we'll be working with for the next twenty years—or those with whom we've been colleagues for the previous twenty years. The feedback we provide isn't honest, or at least it doesn't reflect what's in our brain, heart, and soul. We don't invest in the development of our colleagues unless we are complimenting them on some skill or content expertise. I'm not discounting the importance of that kind of feedback. It's essential and also lacking in most departments of higher education. But in general, we allow our colleagues their weaknesses; we don't challenge them or even suggest that they might need to learn how to hold the attention of the class better or deal more effectively with problem students. When we possess this laissez-faire attitude, our academic departments are less than they should be. A little honest interdepartment feedback could go a long way.

When we give up on someone, we smile at them in the hallway. We will ask them about their holiday plans. We will wish them a happy New Year. But the conversation doesn't get much deeper. Wouldn't it be a step in the right direction if we supported the development of our colleagues, providing the type of honest, just-in-time feedback that could raise their awareness of how they teach and help them improve? Of course, doing so requires courage and the ability to engage in mature, conversational intimacy. It would make all the difference.

Friends

Friendship can be a nebulous term. It's virtually impossible to define what makes a friend, but for me, true friendship involves a covenant, an agreement that absolute trust binds the two together. When we need a friend to provide us with feedback, we don't need five hundred of them. We just need one. I have a luxury in that I have a true friend, Paul, who also happens to be a colleague. When I check in with him when I arrive three hours after he has arrived at school, he looks at me directly in the eyes and tells me what is going on inside of me. He knows whether I'm psychologically ready to face the day or whether I need a pep talk about whether I can succeed in the immediate future. I think I can do the same for him.

He is the first one I talk to after a class goes well or has gone poorly. He is the first one I call at night when I'm stewing on a class plan. He is the first one I tell if I'm depressed about my abilities or my complicated life. He is there to listen, tease me, make sarcastic comments with love as the motivation. Paul is priceless. He doesn't know how to cut corners. He only knows how to live "straight up." He lives his life throwing fast-balls right down the center of the baseball plate. I can't BS him. I can't say one thing and mean another without being confronted with support. Challenge and support. That is what a friend does. A friend will take your edges off. A friend will hold up a mirror and point out the positives and the blemishes. A friend will know which blemishes you are obsessing about.

Partner

Our spouses and significant others know us best, but we don't often take advantage of this knowledge in a strategic, purposeful manner.

Exceptions exist, of course. I've heard of a couple that meets once a month to have a celebration lunch or a gratitude lunch. This couple has been married well over forty years. They are affectionate in public. They hold hands. They hug each other way too much. And they have these lunches where they express appreciation to one another for how they honor each other's dreams. If there is need for a gentle nudge in a particular behavioral direction, they offer it firmly but compassionately. They look in each other's eyes and say what is in their hearts.

For the past five years, during the concluding session with executives who have found themselves attending executive education programs, I ask the executives when was the last time they had a gratitude session with their significant other. I ask, "How many of you have weekly or monthly or semiannual checkups with your partner? How many have structures set up that create sacred time for conversations that are not about logistics? The teaching rooms are silent. Whether there are 150 leaders in the room or 10, the responses in the room are the same. Absolute silence. I have heard from no more than a handful over the years who are strategic in sharing developmental suggestions and appreciation for the other. Not logistics meetings, but meetings of a deeper, higher purpose. Another opportunity to refine self and someone else.

Children

Let me return where we began. When it comes to feedback, the best insights often emerge from the mouths of babes. For those of you who decided at some point in your lives to raise children, you know that they speak truth. They are fearless in telling us what they see and feel. We have various ways of silencing them. In fact, suffering for children begins when we tell them we don't want to hear their collective voices. But they are fearless in staying true to what they experience. Why wouldn't we all want sage wisdom from these wise and naïve individuals? In research on healthy family functioning, the data are clear that family systems are better off when they have ways of giving one another feedback, whether that be through family discussions or family activities. Family members will give you the feedback with love, without edges, without motives.

Teach students that it's acceptable and critical for them to speak up and give their views. Illustrate by example that you experience them as partners in this enterprise called family. Insist they have skin in the game. You will gain insights you never imagined.

Earlier I shared the story of my fifteen-year-old daughter, Sara, when I asked her for feedback. Let me also tell you what transpired when I made the same request of my then four-year-old. "Joanna, what's one thing I could do to be a better dad?" Without hesitation she replied, "Dad, when you are reading stories to me in my bed, when you lie next to me, sometimes you seem so tired. When you are tired you try to skip pages in the book."

And she was right. I would try to deflect her attention. I would skip a couple of pages before she looked back at the book. Apparently it wasn't working. I was caught dead-to-rights. If I'm honest with myself, I know that I was skipping pages in order to get back to my "real work." I wanted to complete the bedtime routines so I could move to my emails, my voicemails. I could get a head start on tomorrow's list of things to accomplish.

While this feedback didn't help me become a better teacher, it did open my eyes to how I hurry through tasks that are important in order to get to other tasks. Am I short-changing my students by doing the same thing? Am I deflecting their attention from my hurry-up mode, failing to provide sufficient attention to subjects that are important to them but that I find less than engaging? Joanna alerted me to this tendency that I might otherwise have missed.

The Relationship Factor

Feedback doesn't take place in a vacuum. Instead, it occurs within the context of relationships. Throughout the book, I've emphasized that horizontal communication patterns are more effective and efficient than vertical relationships. Speaking down to another person—the way a teacher may speak to a student or a boss to an employee—brings only short-term outcomes, and even if you manage to convince someone to change, you'll create long-term resentment (and the change may only be short-lived). The best way to present feedback is with the assumption that the other person is a full and equal partner, increasing feedback's impact.

Research by Adam Grant suggests that feedback is the result of give and take within relationships. Thus, communicating perceptions and feelings with the assumption that the other person is valued changes the nature of the conversation to one where empathy and seeking understanding are central in the interaction. Feedback gains power when people feel valued and understood.

My mentor, Edgar Schein, told me regularly that asking questions was more effective than giving someone else your opinion about behavior. He constantly reminded me that advice conveyed as feedback would fall on deaf ears. Even worse, if the ears weren't deaf, they hear the message and make people angry or defensive. When I give feedback, I try to be aware of what's going on inside of me. In this way, I prevent myself from barking at a student because something about the interaction made me upset. Instead, I try to structure the feedback in a way that the student feels listened to and understood.

Marcus Buckingham and others highlight the importance of focusing on the strengths not weaknesses of others. His research highlights that when we think we are going to get negative feedback, we restrict our thinking and become cautious and worried. Our learning capacity diminishes. Jane Dutton and her colleagues at the University of Michigan emphasize their process called "The Reflected Best Self," positing that we respond to positive more readily than to negative. By pointing out specific behaviors that are positive and useful for more learning, we slow down the process and increase the likelihood that feedback will be perceived as useful rather than as a threat.

What all this boils down to is that the ability to see and hear all the time is crucial for effective feedback. Potentially, data are presented through every instance of feedback and need not be a onetime experience—a formal, sit-down, scheduled, and labeled session with a student. In fact, it takes hundreds of conversations between two people to create the kind of bond where greater trust and empathy are in play, where feedback penetrates our defenses and sticks.

We need not shy away from important conversations or fear feedback, whether as the giver or receiver. However, we do need to remember to emphasize the positive in that feedback so that people feel like its purpose is to help them continue or change to an upward trajectory.

Keep It Coming, Even When It Hurts

Logically, the most accomplished members of our society should be the most open to feedback. After all, we've achieved a lot of success; shouldn't that give us sufficient confidence to solicit and absorb critical comments?

Apparently not. You probably know people—teachers, business leaders, doctors, lawyers—who have been hugely successful but whose egos are so large that they can't tolerate even a whiff of negativity about themselves or how they do their jobs. If these people are lucky, they have systems in place at their jobs that force them to listen to feedback, that provide them with tools and techniques to act on that feedback and become better at what they do.

Teachers often lack effective systems. As I've suggested, many don't pay attention to student evaluations, and scant development processes exist to help them grow as teachers even when they do pay attention. For this reason, they need to seek out feedback from others—colleagues, friends, partners, and their children. They need to take what they hear seriously and figure out how to use the information to change their behaviors.

I write all this with great sincerity, yet I have to ask myself continuously: Do I really want feedback? It continues to pain me when I don't measure up. However, after some reflection, I realize that I'm afraid I won't measure up to myself, to the unrealistic expectations I've created for myself. Thank you to the mirrors in my life who continue to endure my humanness. Keep the feedback coming—and yes, it still hurts. But it also continues to push me in the long struggle upwards called growing.

FOURTEEN

Mr. Rogers

Improving the Teaching Neighborhood

What is essential is invisible to the eye.

—*Antoine de Saint-Exupéry's* The Little Prince

Tony Athos, one of the great Harvard Business School (HBS) professors of organizational behavior and interpersonal behavior, coined the term "an instructor's interlude." This type of interlude describes the process of a teacher who poses a question to the students, pauses, metaphorically steps to the side of his current stance, and answers the question himself. It is a way to highlight a concept, tell a story, or share an insight that has emerged at that very moment in the classroom. The teacher answers the query and steps back into the regular role as teacher.

Here is an example. The class may be in the middle of analyzing why a leader continues to make the same error over and over again relative to judging the quality of her senior team. In the middle of the debate, trying to make sense of what is transpiring with this protagonist, the teacher pauses and asks the question to herself but in reality shares it with the class. The question might be, How do I figure out what my blind spots are after I've been in a system for a long time? The instructor might share how she stumbled in assessing a particular student, how she realized the errors in judgment she had made, and what to do to enhance her effectiveness. After telling the story, the teacher steps back into the discussion about the case at hand.

The essence of this book is to describe an instructor's interlude about preparing, delivering, and learning through the pedagogical process. Why do teachers do what they do when engaging with students in the classroom, when creating and designing a curriculum, and when evaluating students and their work, and how do teachers improve as teachers over time?

But there is a more central reason I wanted to write the book. I felt these instructional interludes offered insightful and at times provocative lessons about what it means to be a teacher. Like Shakespearean asides, they reveal what's really going on in a teacher's mind. Authentic Leadership is one of the courses that I've discussed in these pages. But the questions I've asked in class and that I've examined here are applicable to any teacher and any class subject. I've described what transpires on the classroom stage as well as back stage, hoping to provide an inside perspective on teaching.

I've also drawn a parallel between teachers and leaders—a parallel that I hope teachers will use to draw on the best practices of leaders (and vice versa). I find the similarities between the two professions striking and educational. Both professions require a "personal touch," one that inspires learning and behavior change. Both teachers and leaders are at their best when they're maturely vulnerable; that's when they can make the greatest impact on others.

In the process of writing this book, I've emphasized six key dimensions that are prerequisites for memorable teaching: reassure with content expertise, know the students, be true to style, know how to create a safe learning environment, get out of your own way, and be believable. Let's look at each one, starting with the course content.

Reassure with Content Expertise

Over the years I've found that this fundamental aspect may be the easiest task of all for a teacher. Once you have organized a design for a course, the core preparation is simply time intensive. This should be the easiest because you have already selected this particular area of expertise and inquiry. I chose years earlier that I wanted to focus on organizational behavior and leadership. I should be one of the most informed teachers on campus on these topics.

I selected this area of study because it resonated with me intellectually and emotionally. When I prepare for a class, it is relatively easy to focus because of my initial interest in the topic. The students also give you the benefit of the doubt because they assume you are an expert in the field. Given that you have taught the current population and a particular age range, you know and understand in general terms their knowledge of the content. You know, given the assignments for the day, the context of the subject matter and how the students have gone about studying the material.

You are sharing with them the secrets behind the veil. They must question on occasion whether you are too passionate, too convinced that your topic is the most important topic in the world. You need to convince your audience that they have been invited into this chamber to explore the secrets and mysteries that you will uncover with them. You have to convince them that there is nothing more urgent to you than conveying how important this material is as a foundation for making a difference.

Know the Students

Do I have any understanding of what my students are dealing with day-to-day? Are they worrying about recruiting, or about the upcoming holiday break? If I believe that pacing is crucial, I need to have a sense of where the students are psychologically and emotionally.

While students compare and contrast themselves to one another, I communicate to them my perceptions about who they are and how they're developing throughout the semester to give them an objective reading. By knowing my students, I can offer feedback that may offset their feelings of inferiority to others (even if these feelings are illusory). The challenge is to truly empathize with them during this intense time period.

Let me give you an example of one student who shared with me her mind chatter for the first forty-five seconds beginning when she entered the classroom.

- Class begins in forty-five seconds. I'll go in through the back entrance today. That way I can avoid making eye contact with Emily. It's not that I dislike her. It just feels awkward that we shared dinner together at least once a week last year, and this year we've spoken just twice. Ever since Emily's internship in the fashion industry last summer, she mostly hangs out with the rich kids' group. She's not a bad person. The most down to earth of that crew. It's just that I'd rather not run into her.

- Thirty-five seconds left. I slide into my seat and prop my name card up in front of me. I look to my right to smile at Andrew—a silent attempt at "Good morning." He's on his phone, furiously texting away, and misses my gesture completely. I wonder if a loved one is sick, whether he received a job offer, or if he's got big plans tonight. Speaking of which, what am I doing tonight? I have to figure that out . . .

- **Twenty seconds.** Selfish! You're thinking about evening plans when you still haven't called Grandpa since he had a minor stroke last week. Dad's been reminding you every day. I wonder if all the other grandkids have called, and if he thinks you don't care about him. Too busy at HBS for family. "Call Grandpa," I type into my phone, before hastily turning it off.

- **Ten seconds.** I read the case for today, right? Of course; I always do. But that's not enough here. I have to be ready for the cold call if it comes to me. Bucket my thoughts neatly so I can share them in a compelling way with the class. What buckets would I use for today's case? Goddamn. Why do I never think about this before I walk in the room? Will it be total word vomit if I'm asked to start? My stomach growls. Did I forget breakfast again?

- **Zero seconds.** I place my feet firmly on the ground and scoot my chair up close to the desk, clasping my hands in front of me. I feel my heart rate start to speed up slightly. I exhale slowly in an attempt to bring it back down to normal. Class begins.

I was interested in having a few students record their internal conversations so that I could understand more fully the emotional patterns that the students experience.

Should I feel overwhelmed by the fact that ninety students are monitoring every second of every day? In the process of empathizing with the students, does the thought of their constant mind-racing dialogues discourage me from connecting with them? I have found that the more I learn about them, the more I think I can connect with them because of the spirit that might emanate from me to them. I continue to be naïve enough to believe that I could on a good day have all students mesmerized by the content and the spirit they feel in the classroom. I believe in my bones that the students will remember the course not by the content but because of the feelings that were generated individually and collectively.

Students' past experiences with their Organizational Behavior courses will also inform how they approach my class. I want to know them well enough to get a sense of whether they are enrolling in class because of the positive experiences they've had in their first year or whether they will be suspicious given their prior experiences. I've asked the students to write a one-page document describing why they want to take the course. I also ask what they have heard about the class prior to signing up. I find myself discussing the process that humans have of painting pictures of what something will be like based on little to no evidence. It's a way for me to normalize the various thoughts and feelings that the students may be bringing with them as they enter the class.

At the end of the day, I want students to know that I care about them more than I do about the content. Clearly, I illustrate my care and interest in them by the way I prepare and convince them that this is the best place for them to be right now in their day. Athos reflected how a colleague called from the West Coast who was worried about the following day's opening day with MBAs. Athos listened for a few minutes and then replied, "You're really in trouble. You're so concerned with your own persona as the teacher that you haven't thought about theirs." I want to be at least as aware of the students' concerns as I am of my challenges in dealing with them.

This acknowledgment is a useful transition to the third important dimension in my effort to be the teacher I want to become.

Be True to Style

Earlier in the book, I alluded to core and stylistic patterns that inhibited my journey as a teacher. I highlighted my either/or thinking. I underscored how charming I am as a teacher until I'm not, transforming into a frightening beast right before students' very eyes. I also discussed my willingness to take big risks in the classroom and in life and rest for a time until the next challenge arises. These confessions are painful to see in print. I criticized a younger colleague when I felt like he was more interested in the show he created for students based on impressing them than in the teaching process. I hurt his feelings. However, I could make the observation because I realize even in the twilight of my career that I'm too concerned with me than I should be. The more I can get out of my own way and realize the moments that I've regressed to a teacher-centered approach rather than a student-focused approach, the more powerful the experience will be for the students. I'm humiliated internally when I see my insecure self step up and take over so that the students can see places I shouldn't or wouldn't share on a better day. I feel shame when I believe that a student has paid the price for my obsession with self.

I need to be fully aware of what happens in the classroom that alters my style to the point that learning has been put on hold. I know that side conversations annoy me. Passing notes in class annoys me. Seeing students on phones during class sends me through the roof. I take it very personally if I can't hold the students' attention. I see phones as a personal affront. Students entering class late, and soon thereafter, raising their hands to get in bothers me. Students' communicating across the classroom in any way bothers me. I'm feeling self-conscious even listing the number of behaviors that annoy me. And the irony is that students on my best days describe me as one of the more caring faculty members they've had at the university.

So given that I understand my trip wires, given my love for students, how do I use my style in a way that leverages all of our talents? First, I believe that my motivation is genuine and where it should be. Second, I have a style that communicates interest and connection in others. My assumption is that on any given day there will be surprises in the classroom where I can either put my best self forward or allow the dark side to emerge which typically causes harm to others and to myself.

Create a Safe Learning Environment

Earlier in the chapter, I shared with you the mind chatter of a student for forty-five seconds while entering a classroom. Can you imagine the opportunity a teacher has to manage all those subtexts that are transpiring every second of a class? I've already discussed how to know the subject and students to the point that you can focus on the moment. I mention to every class on the first day of class that my goal is to create a safe but uncomfortable environment. I want the students to be sitting on the edge of their seats, engaged in this learning enterprise. However, they must trust that they are safe during the eighty-minute session.

Students don't want to be embarrassed, surprised, or shamed. They shouldn't arrive with those emotions engulfing them. I must illustrate that even when one of them is not prepared or wastes class time with comments that don't further the conversation, I will be there for every student, not just those who are mini-Toms. While it sounds comforting to have ninety reflections of myself all focused on me, I can't do my work as a teacher if the outcome is a reproduction of me. The class works when each student makes a choice to trust me. Why would the students do that? If they believe I'm interested in the "least of them," if they know that my intentions are pure in that I want to create the best learning opportunity for every one of them, they will sign on. The students must assume that I am on their side in that I want them to learn the material. Most important, I am there to push each student to illustrate courage in whatever form it manifests itself for each student. For one student it may mean raising his hand at the beginning of the class and not waiting until the end of class. For another it may mean disagreeing with another student in front of ninety other students. For another student, courage may mean to be quiet when you know you have the answer, yet you know that another student needs airtime.

My hope is that all students experience the amygdala hijacking their emotions and thoughts and feelings. I want all the students to learn that they can label their affect and feel like they are ahead of the curve, not fainting in front of their classmates. Understanding and experiencing our fears and our reactions to those emotions and feelings is where a manager lives at some point every day. I don't want my students to run from those experiences. Rather I want them to know those experiences will come. But when they do, the students can experience all parts of their emotions and come out the other side alive and stronger.

By connecting one-to-one with each student, I begin to build a context for trust to live and endure. By asking questions outside of class, I illustrate that I'm interested in the student as a person. I'm less interested in the student focused on image management. I'm more inclined to connect with those who are moving closer to who they really are or want to be rather than who or what image they are attempting to sell.

Get Out of Your Own Way

I recognize that I take teaching consciousness to an extreme at times. But I also know that being constantly vigilant has a payoff. I know my patterns can get me in trouble. I've shared some of that trouble earlier, and here I'm going to share some more. I try to get out of my own way, and being vigilant of my patterns is a good preventative.

Still, I experience my share of classroom disasters when I just react to what's happening in class and am not conscious about my patterns. Last winter I was teaching in an executive course, and a classroom incident caused me to hit my anger button. It felt like all my patterns were in play. I was so put off by the condescending nature of the student's comment that I said whatever I could to put down the student. It was one of my worst moments as a teacher in any setting.

"If you can control thousands of employees, you can control your spouse." He seemed serious. The other participants sat in stunned silence.

That was the comment that derailed me. I've thought about my reaction too many times, replaying it on an endless loop. What got into me? What set me off to the point that I humiliated a guest of the school, a participant in one of the HBS executive programs?

Each moment of every minute opens up the possibility for creating an experience that is unforgettable for the student. Each moment creates an opening that can change someone else's life. As I reflect on my response to this executive, I believe that my behavior might have earned me censure from the dean or even a more severe sanction. In each course, I warn students about humiliating other human beings. I tell them that if they embarrass someone, it will come back to haunt them. In this instance, it came back to haunt me. Why does it haunt us if we humiliate someone? Because the humiliated individual reverts to survival mode.

The student must choose between fighting back or leaving the classroom emotionally and psychologically scarred. The amygdala goes into overdrive. The student's heart rate increases. The student worries more about getting out of the situation than about anything else. The student feels so exposed, so naked, so frightened because of the experience and his physical response to it that the student questions whether he will survive the experience. Even though rationally he knows he will survive physically, his amygdala "tells" him that he may not.

I am troubled by these experiences, and I try to prevent them from repeating by being aware of what can set me off. It's not easy. Our patterns are deep seated and often rooted in childhood experiences.

I remember noticing my father fidgeting with his side pocket flap on his sports coat when we were in a tense situation. Dad did two things when getting tense. One, he played with the side pocket. Two, he began grooming his mustache with his fingers. His eyes would be looking out into the distance, or he would be looking down as if in a trance. But the fingers on his right hand would be stroking one side of his mustache, first the right side, then the left side. Back and forth. Slowly, deliberately. Perhaps he was counting to ten to calm down, but I remember him getting to ten quickly.

His temper would go from one to ten in a flash. The moment he began to talk in a hushed, tight tone, I knew I didn't want to experience what would happen. I didn't want to be any part of it. In reality, I didn't worry about my siblings. I worried about what was happening inside me. I could feel my face heating up.

Like my father, I was powerless to step to the side when the student said, "If you can control thousands of employees, you can control your spouse." If I had been more conscious, I might have gained power over my behavior. Unfortunately, it was one of those times when I just reacted. In the moment I verbally attacked a student, I lost the whole class. It could have been just for a moment or forever. Even though a large proportion of the class agreed with my assessment of the situation, I lost them anyway. I lost them because they weren't sure whether they could ever trust me not to turn on them. I don't blame them for experiencing fear and trembling here at HBS. After I apologized the following morning, I could see the class lost a bit of its tension. But even though I personally apologized to the one student, he never wanted to make contact with me again. I lost him because of my fear and my worries about my image as the person controlling and managing a classroom. This doesn't happen often. But when it does, I beat myself up over my inability to get out of my own way.

Be Believable

The power of authenticity as a teacher and manager cannot be overstated. At every turn, students want to understand with whom they are creating that covenantal relationship that I've described earlier in this book. The question is whether or not the instructor transcends the message. This phenomenon is at the very core of what differentiates good and great teachers.

As I read Bruce Springsteen's autobiography, titled *Born to Run* (2016), the author describes the battle between his multiple selves. "It's like driving along in a car with all the characters that add up to create me. I want the responsible, creative, caring Bruces to have their hands on the wheel. Yet all the other personalities and characteristics keep fighting to get a turn driving the car" (p. 228).

Using a different metaphor, I refer to my daughter Sara's analogy of the Knights of the Round Table. Sara is a psychiatrist at a medical center in the Rocky Mountains. She often refers to the internal conflicts that the various knights have with one another to control her behavior. Sara, like Springsteen, sees this internal battle as part of everyday life. They both emphasize that the right characters don't always get their way. Through a sense of surrender and self-acceptance and humor, it's more likely that the right Saras and Bruces and Toms will win the battles.

Being believable is accepting the internal struggle as part of life and being aware enough to make sure the right person maintains control in the classroom. Knowing the patterns that undermine the right person is crucial. In real time, during a class period, the good teacher will feel the irresponsible personas taking over the proverbial wheel. Label what is transpiring, and acknowledge it. Then return control to the better part of us, the most authentic and believable part.

None of this is easy for teachers. All of us struggle with self-doubt throughout the day. We create narratives for ourselves that knock us off center, that prevent us from being believable, from knowing our students, from getting out of our own way. To maintain our center, let me share some wisdom from my best friend.

My Best Friend

My best friend, Paul, has written on his whiteboard a list titled "Words Are Powerful Things." These phrases have become part of his ritual on teaching days. He says the phrases over and over again. He struggles to ensure that the right hands are on the steering wheel. I share his mantra with the reader:

Words Are Powerful Things

I am accomplished
I am hard working
I am blessed
I am fortunate
I am prepared
I am confident
I am capable
I am enough
I am a problem solver
I am a good friend
I am creative
I am bold
I am resilient
I can do hard things
I am strong
I am determined
I have faith
I have all I need
I am valuable
I am successful
I am a fighter
I can handle it

I am smart

I can focus

I am loved

The profession of teaching can be torturous. Remaining believable to self and others is the most important dimension of the teaching endeavor. Nothing can beat the power of believing in self and communicating that by your very essence. I am in awe of my friend. I'm in awe because of his commitment to being the best person he can be. Every class period is a litmus test to determine whether or not Paul has "it." When he isn't teaching, he's obsessing and perseverating about whether or not he has the right content, the right context, and the right style and whether or not the students are committed to him based on who he is and how they experience him.

Besides the six fundamental themes that I've noted here and discussed throughout the book, I'd like to leave you with three questions that are relevant to teachers at every level and in every type of educational setting.

The Three Guiding Questions

When I first joined the HBS faculty, there were three fundamental questions that I believed could guide my endeavors to be authentic and genuine. They became guideposts when I felt I had lost my way, when I had rationalized my behavior to fit my mood or situation. I've used these questions as guardrails during these twenty years of self-discovery through the classroom experience at Harvard.

1. How do I experience others? What are my beliefs about why humans do what they do? This question pushes me to reflect on not only how I believe I'm motivated but how I believe students are motivated as well. If I try to consider the answer to this

question, I have to face myself and confront whether or not my actions are in line with those beliefs.

For example, if I believe students and children and friends grow through challenges and aspirational goals and being supported through those experiences, I have to ask myself whether or not I really do support students and follow up with appropriate support at the appropriate time. It is a two-step process. One step alone won't do. So this simple question about how I experience others as trusting, as devious, as lazy, or as goal driven will inform how I interact every day with those with whom I come into contact.

2. How do others experience me? This second reflection puts into play to what extent I am aware of how others see me in myriad contexts and in myriad relationships. In asking myself this fundamental question, I have to ask myself whether I spend more time selling a particular image of myself to others through my interactions with them or whether I allow myself to be me right down to the core. Have I collected enough information through the years to have a sense of self and what and how I'm portraying myself to others?

This developmental process suggests that I'm continually seeking outside feedback so that I don't allow my self-authored narratives to be distorted over time by my biases and blind spots. I do know that if I don't create structures in my life to force me to receive information about my presence and persona, I will slip into patterns where I don't want to hear how others experience me. If I don't set up specific time each month to chat with my partner about how we are honoring each other's dreams, I won't initiate this type of interaction. The only way to stay attuned to how others experience me is to ask and be curious, even if it may be surprising and perhaps painful.

3. How do others experience themselves when they are in your presence? This is the key question in the context of understanding

believability in teaching, in managing, in leading, in parenting, in enhancing relationships. This question has come back to me through former students writing to me and reminding me of the question. It has returned to me in student evaluations when students are asked what they will remember from the course. It boomerangs back through follow-up interactions with participants in our executive education courses.

Mr. Rogers and Believability

In the late 1960s, Mr. Fred Rogers introduced a children's television program through the Public Broadcasting Service (PBS). Older kids would mock and mimic him. *Saturday Night Live* had an ongoing heyday parodying his every move, from buttoning up his cardigan sweater (knitted by his mother) to taking off his black, low-cut Keds. I must admit that I found myself on occasion not knowing what to do with my feelings and reactions to this low-key, earnest producer-songwriter. Over time Mr. Rogers grew on me to the point that after my kids moved on developmentally, I continued to be enamored of his tone, his pacing, his sequencing of experiences on the screen, and his overall calming manner.

Mr. Rogers wanted to teach children another way to love themselves and accept themselves. He taught children to be kind to self and others. His program was the antidote to other kids' programming that was founded on high-energy, fast-paced constant movement and distraction. There was no calming effect to these other programs.

Over the years Mr. Rogers began to evolve into a cult hero of sorts. He couldn't go to visit New York City without security because so many children wanted to touch him and hear him and be close to him. Over time I became a fan because of the way he taught and how I experienced myself in his presence through TV as the medium.

On my fiftieth birthday (at the turn of the century), *Esquire* magazine had Mr. Rogers on the cover with an in-depth article that exposed us all to what made Fred Rogers such a major figure for children everywhere. We all settled down when we heard him.

Sara, my oldest daughter, wrote to Mr. Rogers and expressed how much he meant to her dad. She asked him to sign a cover of the *Esquire* article. He wrote, "To Professor DeLong, won't you be my neighbor, signed Mr. Fred Rogers."

This gift so moved me that I wrote Mr. Rogers a thank you note expressing how much he had meant to me. I mentioned that I found myself experiencing my own emotions when I heard him, read his words, and experienced him in some way.

A month later Mr. Rogers responded with a personal note to me. I share it with you on the next page.

I began this section of the chapter on believability with a quote from *The Little Prince*. The quote was taken from a book written by Fred Rogers (*You Are Special*, 1994). Through this mysterious phenomenon of communicating on a different level with another human, both individuals can be lifted up so that both feel special. That is the essence of the true teaching experience. There is no wavering. It is straight and right and true. It is the simple truth that what is essential is invisible to the eye but not to the spirit.

Ending Where We Began

Jack Gabarro, a mentor and friend, once articulated the opportunities and challenges of teaching. "Each time I teach, I like to start with the hope that I'll be privileged again to experience the awe of connecting. When a comment, a look or something shared alters another's life it's a very touching thing." There are moments of silence when I sit quietly with my friend and colleague Scott Snook and share the times that

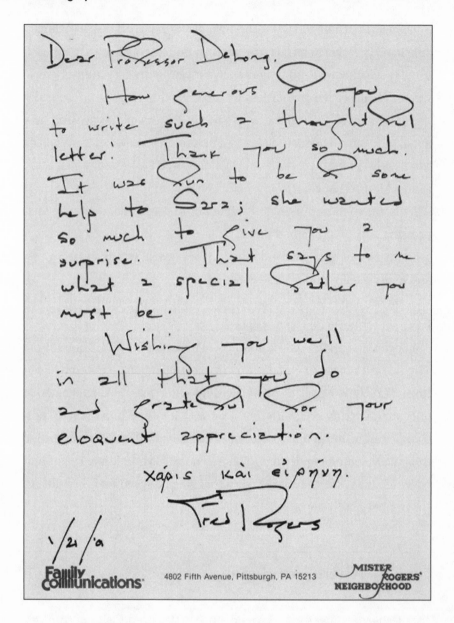

Dear Professor DeLong,

How generous of you to write such a thoughtful letter! Thank you so much. It was fun to be of some help to Sara; she wanted so much to give you a surprise. That says to me what a special Father you must be.

Wishing you well in all that you do and grateful for your eloquent appreciation.

χάρις καὶ εἰρήνη.

Fred Rogers

1/21/'0

Family Communications·   4802 Fifth Avenue, Pittsburgh, PA 15213   MISTER ROGERS' NEIGHBORHOOD

make it all worth it. As a collective bunch of teachers, we often are reluctant to share when we have one of those moments that validate our efforts to jump into the deep end of teaching.

In a conversation with Gabarro, he reflected that we need to "aim to teach as an art, settle if we make it craft, and support one another when we find ourselves lowering our craft to a science." Every second in the classroom affords us the opportunity to avail ourselves to a combination of our thoughts, feelings, impulses, and impressions, so we can create that moment for a student that changes the direction of a life. There is no more worthy profession.

I want to be great, not good. I want every student who experiences me integrating the aforementioned characteristics to leave the room feeling and thinking, "I've got to tell someone else that they have to experience a class facilitated by Tom." Above all, I want them to leave the classroom wanting more of whatever they felt during that eighty-minute session. That only happens if all students experience themselves in a way that challenges them to be more accepting, more aware, and more committed to be all they can be.

Preparing for Difficult Conversations

What Happened

STORIES	IMPACT/INTENT	CONTRIBUTION
What is my story (e.g., information, experience, rules)?	My intentions Impact on me	What did I contribute to the problem?
What is their story?	Their intentions Impact on them	What did they contribute?

Feelings

What feelings underline my attributions and judgments?

Identity Issues

How does what happened threaten my identity?
What is at stake for me about me?

Crucial Conversations

Todd McKenna was having a hard time paying attention. A third-year associate at Sutherland Brown, Todd was sitting in his boss's office with three other bankers who were going over the final pages for a presentation they would be flying to Chicago to present the next morning. He knew he should pay attention so he could ask any questions he had now, because none of his colleagues would be around when he was making those changes to the document in the unearthly predawn hours. But he was too angry to care right now. Bonuses had been announced earlier in the week, and Todd's boss, Scott Lang, who was a managing director at Sutherland Brown and head of the Consumer Products Group, had told him confidentially he would be the top-paid associate in the class.

But just before this meeting, Todd had been sitting in his bullpen talking with some of the other associates, and some numbers were discussed that made Todd realize it was not true—he was not the top-paid associate. His boss had lied to him, and Todd wondered whether Scott took him to be a fool, thinking he would never find out. Just because Todd didn't act out as much as some of the other associates, Scott probably thought he could pay him less and he wouldn't complain.

Well, Todd was tired of being the perfect associate who kept his head down and just did perfect work. If Scott didn't appreciate him, he knew plenty of other managing directors in the other industry groups who had tried to poach him, and they would be willing to pay him what he was worth.

As the meeting broke up, the three other bankers gathered their papers and walked out, leaving Todd alone in Scott's office. Scott lobbed a pen cap at Todd and said, "McKenna, are you in outer space? What's up with you?"

Todd: Well, if you really want to know, I'm thinking of leaving the group.

Scott: Whoa, where did that come from?

Todd: It might be time for a change—there are some exciting new deals happening in the Energy Group and I know they need associates with experience, so I could add a lot of value.

Scott: If you feel like you need a change, I won't stop you from pursuing exciting new opportunities. But, not only are you adding a lot of value for us in this group, the work is beginning to roll on in here, so the sky's the limit for great associates like you.

Todd: How much value?

Scott: Well, Todd, you know I've told you before that you do great work. I don't think I was half as knowledgeable when I was a third-year associate, so you are on your way to having a very productive career.

Todd: But Scott, you say that to everyone.

Scott: What is that supposed to mean?

Todd: The other associates all think you love them, and they're doing a great job too.

Scott: Well, we do have a good group of associates this year, which I have to say is a relief for me—otherwise the bankers complain to me day and night.

Todd: Even Patrick, who we all know flaked when the Munson deal was at a really crucial stage?

Scott: Is that what you've all been saying about him? It'd be nice if you cut your colleagues a little slack. Patrick had a serious health problem that got diagnosed during that deal, and it's amazing he managed to show up at all. But now we're off on a tangent: what are you really trying to ask me?

Todd: Aren't there differences between all of us, in terms of our performance?

Scott: Of course there are, Todd, and I can tell you honestly—you are performing at the top of our expectations. We are really very pleased with you in the group.

Todd: Then why didn't I get paid that way?

Scott: You *did* get paid that way—I lobbied for you to be right at the top of our range.

Todd: Scott, why can't you be straight with me? How can I be at the top of the range if Alan Craine is getting more than I'm getting?

Scott: You're putting me in an awkward situation, Todd. You really shouldn't expect me to discuss other people's compensation with you.

Todd: Are you telling me that Alan is not getting more than I'm getting?

Scott: I'm telling you that you're comparing apples to oranges. Alan should get paid more than you; we're underpaying him as it is—he took a pay cut and a title cut to join us this year when we hired him away from White Hedges. We wanted to build in a year to give him a chance to come up to speed on our way of doing business, before he had production pressure as an officer. But we paid him enough to signal to him that he's on the right track. It's a completely different situation.

Todd: It still looks to everyone else like he did better than I did.

Scott: You're going to have to stop worrying about how things look, or you won't last very long in this business. So basically you were willing to leave my group, and here I was feeling bad thinking we're not creating enough exciting opportunities for you, but really it all comes down to money, and ego, in the end.

Todd: No, it wasn't just money. I felt like you weren't playing straight with me, and I thought I knew you.

Scott: But you didn't trust me very much, clearly. You didn't even come straight out and ask me what you wanted to ask, and you certainly already thought you knew what the truth was anyway. I try hard to be a good manager and to be fair, but I guess that doesn't matter to you.

Todd: Look, Scott, I'm sorry this all came up.

Scott: No, I'm glad it came up. I think it is true that our deal flow has been slow lately, and there might be more going on in the Energy Group. I think it might really make more sense for your career for you to go add value over there. If you'll excuse me, I've got to make some calls before I head out to Chicago.

Todd exits Scott's office.

Professor Thomas J. DeLong and Research Associate Vineeta Vijayaraghavan prepared this case. The company mentioned in the case is fictional.

Achor, Shawn. *The Happiness Advantage: The Seven Principles of Positive Psychology That Fuel Success and Performance at Work*. New York: Crown Business, 2010.

Allison, Graham T. *Essence of Decision: Explaining the Cuban Missile Crisis*. Boston: Little, Brown and Company, 1971.

Andersen, Espen, and Bill Schiano. *Teaching with Cases: A Practical Guide*. Boston: Harvard Business Review Press, 2014.

The Arbinger Institute. *The Anatomy of Peace: Resolving the Heart of Conflict*. San Francisco: Berrett-Koehler, 2015.

———. *Leadership and Self-Deception*. San Francisco: Berrett-Koehler, 2000.

Argyris, Chris. *Reasoning, Learning, and Action: Individual and Organizational*. San Francisco: Jossey-Bass, 1982.

Athos, Anthony G., and John J. Gabarro. *Interpersonal Behavior: Communication and Understanding in Relationships*. Englewood Cliffs, NJ: Prentice-Hall, 1978.

Bain, Ken. *What the Best College Teachers Do*. Cambridge, MA: Harvard University Press, 2004.

Bardwick, Judith M. *Danger in the Comfort Zone: From Boardroom to Mailroom—How to Break the Entitlement Habit That's Killing American Business*. New York: American Management Association, 1995.

Barsh, Joanna, and Susie Cranston. *How Remarkable Women Lead: The Breakthrough Model for Work and Life*. New York: Crown, 2009.

Beckhard, Richard. *Agent of Change: My Life, My Practice*. San Francisco: Jossey-Bass, 1997.

———. *Organization Development: Strategies and Models*. Reading, MA: Addison-Wesley, 1969.

Bellah, Robert N., et al. *Habits of the Heart: Individualism and Commitment in American Life*. Berkeley: University of California Press, 1985.

Bolman, Lee G., and Terrence E. Deal. *Leading with Soul: An Uncommon Journey of Spirit*. San Francisco: Jossey-Bass, 1995.

Borba, Michele. *Unselfie: Why Empathetic Kids Succeed in Our All-about-Me World*. New York: Touchstone, 2017.

Brandon, Craig. *The Five-Year Party: How Colleges Have Given Up on Educating Your Child and What You Can Do about It.* Dallas, TX: BenBella Books, 2010.

Brooks, David. *The Social Animal.* New York: Random House, 2011.

Broughton, Philip Delves. *Ahead of the Curve: Two Years at Harvard Business School.* New York: Penguin Press, 2008.

Brown, Brené. *Daring Greatly: How the Courage to Be Vulnerable Transforms the Way We Live, Love, Parent, and Lead.* New York: Gotham Books, 2012.

———. *Rising Strong.* New York: Spiegel & Grau, 2015.

Byock, Ira. *Four Things That Matter Most.* New York: ATRIA Books, 2014.

Cameron, Kim. *Practicing Positive Leadership: Tools and Techniques That Create Extraordinary Results.* San Francisco: Berrett-Koehler Publishers, 2013.

Christensen, Clay, James Allworth, and Karen Dillon. "Just This Once." In *How Will You Measure Your Life?*, edited by Clayton Christensen, James Allworth, and Karen Dillon. New York: Harper Business Press, 2012.

Clark, D. Cecil, and Beverly Romney Cutler. *Teaching: An Introduction.* San Diego: Harcourt Brace Jovanovich, 1990.

Coles, Robert. *Lives of Moral Leadership: Men and Women Who Have Made a Difference.* New York: Random House Trade Paperbacks, 2000.

Collins, Jim, and Morten T. Hansen. *Great by Choice: Uncertainty, Chaos, and Luck—Why Some Thrive Despite Them All.* New York: Harper Business, 2011.

Cousins, Norman. *The Healing Heart: Antidotes to Panic and Helplessness.* New York: W. W. Norton, 1983.

Csikszentmihalyi, Mihaly. *Flow: The Psychology of Optimal Experience.* New York: Harper & Row, 1990.

———. *Good Business: Leadership, Flow, and the Making of Meaning.* New York: Viking, 2003.

Damasio, Antonio. *The Feeling of What Happens: Body and Emotion in the Making of Consciousness.* San Diego, CA: Harcourt, 1999.

Dealing with Difficult People. Results-Driven Manager Series. Boston: Harvard Business Review Press, 2005.

DeLong, Thomas J. *Flying without a Net: Turn Fear of Change into Fuel for Success.* Boston: Harvard Business School Press, 2011.

DeLong, Thomas J., and Sara DeLong. "The Paradox of Excellence." *Harvard Business Review*, June 2011.

DeLong, Thomas J., John J. Gabarro, and Robert J. Lees. *When Professionals Have to Lead: A New Model for High Performance.* Boston: Harvard Business School Press, 2007.

DeLong, Thomas J., and Vineeta Vijayaraghavan. "Let's Hear It for B Players." *Harvard Business Review*, June 2003.

Dill, David D. *What Teachers Need to Know: The Knowledge, Skills, and Values Essential to Good Teaching.* San Francisco: Jossey-Bass, 1990.

Dirkswager, Edward J. *Teachers as Owners: A Key to Revitalizing Public Education.* Lanham, MD: Scarecrow Press, 2002.

Duhigg, Charles. *The Power of Habit: Why We Do What We Do in Life and Business.* New York: Random House, 2012.

Dweck, Carol S. *Mindset: The New Psychology of Success.* 2008 Ballantine Books Trade Paperback ed. New York: Ballantine Books, 2008.

Eble, Kenneth E. *The Craft of Teaching.* 2nd ed. San Francisco: Jossey-Bass, 1988.

Edmondson, Amy, and D. Smith. "Too Hot to Handle? How to Manage Relationship Conflict." *California Management Review* 49, no. 1 (2006): 6–31.

Edmundson, Mark. *Self and Soul: A Defense of Ideals.* Cambridge, MA: Harvard University Press, 2015.

Eliot, George. *Middlemarch.* Berlin: Asher, 1872.

Farr, Steven. *Teaching as Leadership: The Highly Effective Teacher's Guide to Closing the Achievement Gap.* San Francisco: Jossey-Bass, 2010.

Freire, Paulo. *Teachers as Cultural Workers: Letters to Those Who Dare Teach.* Translated by Donaldo Macedo, Dale Koike, and Alexandre Oliveira. Boulder: Westview Press, 1998.

Friedman, Stewart D. *Total Leadership: Be a Better Leader, Have a Richer Life.* Boston: Harvard Business Review Press, 2008.

Gabarro, J. Personal interview with Thomas DeLong, Boston, MA, June 4, 2010.

Gardner, Howard, and Emma Laskin. *Leading Minds: An Anatomy of Leadership.* New York: Basic Books, 1995.

George, Bill. *True North: Discover Your Authentic Leadership.* San Francisco: Jossey-Bass, 2007.

George, Bill, et al. "Discovering Your Authentic Leadership." *Harvard Business Review,* February 2007, 129–138.

Gilligan, Carol. *In a Different Voice: Psychological Theory and Women's Development.* Cambridge, MA: Harvard University Press, 1982.

Gino, Francesca. *Sidetracked: Why Our Decisions Get Derailed, and How We Can Stick to the Plan.* Boston: Harvard Business Review Press, 2013.

Goffman, Erving. *The Presentation of Self in Everyday Life.* New York: Anchor Books, 1959.

Golden, Daniel. *The Price of Admission: How America's Ruling Class Buys Its Way into Elite Colleges—and Who Gets Left Outside the Gates.* New York: Crown Publishers, 2006.

Goleman, Daniel. *Working with Emotional Intelligence.* New York: Bantam, 1998.

Gottman, John. *Why Marriages Succeed or Fail . . . and How You Can Make Yours Last.* New York: Simon & Schuster Paperbacks, 1994.

Gottman, John, and Nan Silver. *What Makes Love Last? How to Build Trust and Avoid Betrayal.* New York: Simon & Schuster Paperbacks, 2012.

Grant, Adam. *Give and Take.* New York: Penguin Group, 2013.

Groysberg, Boris, and Michael Slind. "Leadership Is a Conversation." *Harvard Business Review,* June 2012, 76–84.

———. *Talk, Inc.: How Trusted Leaders Use Conversation to Power Their Organizations.* Boston: Harvard Business Review Press, 2012.

Handy, Charles. *The Age of Paradox.* Boston: Harvard Business Review Press, 1994.

Hansen, Morten T. *Collaboration: How Leaders Avoid the Traps, Create Unity, and Reap Big Results.* Boston: Harvard Business School Press, 2009.

Joyner, James. "Why Men Can't Have It All, Either." *The Atlantic,* June 2012.

Kanter, Rosabeth Moss. *Confidence: How Winning Streaks & Losing Streaks Begin & End.* New York: Crown Business, 2004.

Kaplan, Robert S. *What You're Really Meant to Do: A Road Map for Reaching Your Unique Potential.* Boston: Harvard Business Review Press, 2013.

Katie, Byron, and Stephen Mitchell. *Loving What Is: Four Questions That Can Change Your Life.* New York: Harmony, 2002.

Katzenbach, Jon R. *Why Pride Matters More Than Money: The Power of the World's Greatest Motivational Force.* New York: Crown Business, 2003.

Kegan, Robert. "The Constitutions of the Self." In *The Evolving Self,* 74–110. Cambridge, MA: Harvard University Press, 1982.

Kegan, Robert, and Lisa Lahey. "The Real Reason People Won't Change." *Harvard Business Review,* November 2001, 84–92.

Kegan, Robert, and Lisa Laskow Lahey. "What Do You Really Want . . . And What Will You Do to Keep from Getting It?" In *How the Way We Talk Can Change the Way We Work,* 1–10. San Francisco: Jossey-Bass, 2001.

Kember, David, and Carmel McNaught. *Enhancing University Teaching: Lessons from Research Into Award-Winning Teachers.* Abingdon, UK: Routledge, 2007.

Khurana, Rakesh. *Searching for a Corporate Savior: The Irrational Quest for Charismatic CEOs.* Princeton, NJ: Princeton University Press, 2002.

Kotter, John P., and Lorne A. Whitehead. *Buy-In: Saving Your Good Idea from Getting Shot Down.* Boston: Harvard Business Review Press, 2010.

Lambert, Craig. *Shadow Work: The Unpaid, Unseen Jobs That Fill Your Day.* Berkeley, CA: Counterpoint, 2015.

Lamott, Anne. *Small Victories: Spotting Improbable Moments of Grace.* New York: Penguin Group, 2014.

Lawrence, Paul R., and Nitin Nohria. *Driven: How Human Nature Shapes Our Choices.* San Francisco: Jossey-Bass, 2002.

Lehrer, J. *A Book about Love*. New York: Simon & Schuster Paperbacks, 2017.

Levin, Barbara B. *Case Studies of Teacher Development: An In-Depth Look at How Thinking About Pedagogy Develops Over Time*. New York: Lawrence Erlbaum Associates, 2003.

Lorsch, Jay W., and Thomas J. Tierney. *Aligning the Stars: How to Succeed When Professionals Drive Results*. Boston: Harvard Business School Press, 2002.

Manzoni, Jean-François, and Jean-Louis Barsoux. "The Set-Up-to-Fail Syndrome." *Harvard Business Review*, March 1998.

Maslansky, Michael, Scott West, Gary DeMoss, and David Saylor. *The Language of Trust: Selling Ideas in a World of Skeptics*. New York: Prentice Hall Press, 2010.

Maté, Gabor, and Gordon Neufeld. *Hold On to Your Kids: Why Parents Need to Matter More Than Peers*. New York: Ballantine Books, 2006.

McKeachie, Wilbert J. *Teaching Tips: A Guidebook for the Beginning College Teacher*. Eighth ed. Lexington, MA: D.C. Heath and Company, 1986.

Miller, Arthur. *Death of a Salesman: Text and Criticism*. Rev. ed. Edited by Gerald Weales. New York: Pengiun Books, 1996.

National Research Council. *How People Learn: Brain, Mind, Experience and School*. Exp. ed. Washington, DC: National Academy Press, 2000.

Naumes, William, and Margaret J. Naumes. *The Art & Craft of Case Writing*. Third ed. Armonk, NY: M. E. Sharpe, 2012.

Nyquist, Jody D., Robert D. Abbott, and Donald H. Wulff, eds. *Teaching Assistant Training in the 1990s*. San Francisco: Jossey-Bass, 1989.

Palmer, Parker J. *The Courage to Teach: Exploring the Inner Landscape of a Teacher's Life*. San Francisco: John Wiley & Sons, 2007.

Parsloe, Eric, and Melville Leedham. *Coaching and Mentoring: Practical Conversations to Improve Learning*. Second ed. Philadelphia: Kogan Page, 2009.

Patterson, Kerry, Joseph Grenny, Ron McMillan, and Al Switzler. *Crucial Conversations: Tools for Talking When Stakes Are High*. New York: McGraw-Hill, 2002.

Pausch, Randy, and Jeffrey Zaslow. *The Last Lecture*. New York: Hyperion, 2008.

Perlow, Leslie A. *Sleeping with Your Smartphone: How to Break the 24/7 Habit and Change the Way You Work*. Boston: Harvard Business Review Press, 2012.

———. *When You Say Yes but Mean No: How Silencing Conflict Wrecks Relationships and Companies . . . and What You Can Do about It*. New York: Crown Business, 2003.

Perlow, Leslie A., and J. L. Porter. "Making Time Off Predictable—And Required." *Harvard Business Review*, October 2009, 102–109.

Petriglieri, Gianpiero, et al. "Up Close and Personal: Building Foundations for Leaders' Development through the Personalization of Management Learning." *Academy of Management Learning and Education* 10, no. 3 (September 2011): 430.

Pfeffer, Jeffrey. *Leadership BS: Fixing Workplace and Careers One Truth at a Time.* New York: HarperCollins, 2015.

Piper, Thomas R., Mary C. Gentile, and Sharon Daloz Parks. *Can Ethics Be Taught? Perspectives, Challenges, and Approaches at Harvard Business School.* Boston: Harvard Business School Press, 1993.

Porter, Lyman W., and Lawrence E. McKibbin. *Management Education and Development: Drift or Thrust into the 21st Century?* New York: McGraw-Hill, 1988.

Quinn, Robert E. *Beyond Rational Management: Mastering the Paradoxes and Competing Demands of High Performance.* San Francisco: Jossey-Bass, 1988.

Riesman, David, Nathan Glazer, and Reuel Denney. *The Lonely Crowd: A Study of the Changing American Character.* Abr. ed. New Haven, CT: Yale University Press, 1969.

Roethlisberger, F. J. *The Elusive Phenomena: An Autobiographical Account of My Work in the Field of Organizational Behavior at the Harvard Business School.* Edited by George F. F. Lombard. Boston: Division of Research, Graduate School of Business Administration, Harvard University; distributed by Harvard University Press, 1977.

Rosovsky, Henry. *The University: An Owner's Manual.* New York: W. W. Norton & Company, 1990.

Rowling, J. K. Commencement speech, Harvard University, 2008.

Ruiz, Don Miguel. *The Four Agreements: A Practical Guide to Personal Freedom.* San Rafael, CA: Amber-Allen, 1997.

Sandberg, Sheryl, and Adam M. Grant. *Option B: Facing Adversity, Building Resilience, and Finding Joy.* New York: Knopf, 2017.

Schein, Edgar H. *Coercive Persuasion: A Socio-Psychological Analysis of the "Brainwashing" of American Civilian Prisoners by the Chinese Communists.* New York: W. W. Norton & Company, 1961.

———. *Helping: How to Offer, Give, and Receive Help.* San Francisco: Berrett-Koehler, 2009.

———. *Humble Inquiry: The Gentle Art of Asking Instead of Telling.* San Francisco: Berrett-Koehler, 2013.

———. *Process Consultation: Lessons for Managers and Consultants.* Vol. II. Reading, MA: Addison-Wesley, 1987.

———. "What to Observe in a Group." In *Reading Book for Human Relations Training*, edited by L. Porter, and B. Mohr, 72–74. Silver Spring, MD: NTL Institute, 1982.

Seligman, Martin E. P. *Learned Optimism: How to Change Your Mind and Your Life*. New York: Pocket Books, 1998.

Simon, Herbert A. *Administrative Behavior: A Study of Decision-Making Processes in Administrative Organization*. 2nd ed. New York: Free Press, 1957.

Slaughter, Anne-Marie. "Why Women Still Can't Have It All." *The Atlantic*, July–August, 2012.

Smith, Diana McLain. *The Elephant in the Room: How Relationships Make or Break the Success of Leaders and Organizations*. San Francisco: Jossey-Bass, 2011.

Smith, Kenwyn K., and David N. Berg. *Paradoxes of Group Life: Understanding Conflict, Paralysis, and Movement in Group Dynamics*. San Francisco: Jossey-Bass, 1987.

Snook, Scott A. *Friendly Fire: The Accidental Shootdown of U.S. Black Hawks over Northern Iraq*. Princeton, NJ: Princeton University Press, 2000.

Snook, Scott A., Nitin Nohria, and Rakesh Khurana, eds. *The Handbook for Teaching Leadership: Knowing, Doing, and Being*. Los Angeles: Sage, 2012.

Soloveitchik, Joseph B. *The Lonely Man of Faith*. New Milford, CT: Maggid Books, 2012.

Solway, David. *Education Lost: Reflections on Contemporary Pedagogical Practice*. Toronto: Ontario Institute for Studies in Education Press, 1989.

Springsteen, Bruce. *Born to Run*. New York: Simon & Schuster, 2016.

Steele, Claude M. *Whistling Vivaldi: And How Other Clues to How Stereotypes Affect Us*. New York: W. W. Norton & Company, 2010.

Stone, Douglas, Bruce Patton, and Sheila Heen. *Difficult Conversations: How to Discuss What Matters Most*. 10th anniv. ed. New York: Penguin Books, 2010.

Storr, Anthony. *The Essential Jung*. Princeton, NJ: Princeton University Press, 1983.

Sukhomlinsky, Vasily. *To Children I Give My Heart*. Translated by Holly Smith. Moscow: Progress Publishers, 1981.

Sutton, Robert I. *Good Boss, Bad Boss: How to Be the Best . . . and Learn from the Worst*. New York: Business Plus, 2010.

Thorne, Kaye, and David Mackey. *Everything You Ever Needed to Know about Training*. 3rd ed. London: Kogan Page, 2005.

Turkle, Sherry. *Alone Together: Why We Expect More from Technology and Less from Each Other*. New York: Basic Books, 2011.

———. *Reclaiming Conversation: The Power of Talk in a Digital Age*. New York: Penguin Press, 2015.

Yeşil, Magdalena, and Sara Grace. *Power Up: How Smart Women Win in the New Economy*. New York: Seal Press, 2017.

Yourcenar, Marguerite. *Memoirs of Hadrian; and, Reflections on the Composition of Memories of Hadrian*. Translated by Grace Frick. New York: Farrar, Straus and Giroux, 2005.

ACKNOWLEDGMENTS

As I finished teaching the final class of the semester in 1977, while I was in graduate school, one of the freshman students approached me and shared, "Every time I've looked at you during the course, you've reminded me of Herman Munster from *The Munsters*."

Why begin an acknowledgments section with such a memory? I want to acknowledge the students over the past forty-three years who have provided me with the fuel for the refiner's fire of my development. Every class taught over these decades has provided the conditions for learning how to teach. So my students deserve the primary acknowledgment for this constant reminder of my human condition.

As an elementary school student, I experienced the hypnotic powers of Mr. Stickel and Mr. Snively. In graduate school, I witnessed Bonner Ritchie and Stephen Covey use metaphor to hold their students captive.

As I began to teach, it was my close friend Paul McKinnon who showed me ways to be more precise in my course design. We taught side by side in various environments, pushing each other to take risks in the classroom. His support has been a constant from the beginning.

While I was teaching at Brigham Young University, Hal Miller, Elouise Bell, and William Bradshaw modeled how to expect more from students.

Joining the faculty at Harvard Business School (HBS) was like jumping into the deep end of a pool. Everywhere I turned, I saw excellence in the classroom. Faculty not only know content but also understand process.

Len Schlesinger, a mentor and friend, told me early on to "love the content and the students." That wise counsel has been with me since the first time I set foot on the HBS campus. The Service Management Department treated me like family in my early years at HBS.

Ashish Nanda, a friend and colleague, taught me about curriculum design in the early stages of developing our course on professional service firms. He has developed into one of the most gifted teachers I've ever observed.

Other faculty at HBS have influenced how I view the teaching profession. The list is too long to mention them all.

Nitin Nohria has spent hours reading this manuscript in detail and providing feedback that enhanced the book. I left every meeting wanting to raise my sights to do better.

Scott Snook has been my partner in crime as I've transitioned to our course on leadership development.

Jack Gabarro is responsible for my taking on the task of writing this book. He is the one person who consistently encouraged me to capture on paper what I try to create in the classroom. Jack introduced me to the legacy of Professor Tony Athos here at the Business School. Jack would watch me teach and tell me how much I reminded him of Tony and the atmosphere he created for learning in the classroom. Tony is one of those individuals I can't wait to meet in the next life.

Willis Emmons, Director of the Christensen Center for Teaching and Learning, has spent countless hours analyzing my patterns and processes in the classroom. Dakota Robinson, faculty support specialist, has worked conscientiously to keep me organized through the process of writing and teaching. My editor Bruce Wexler has been my guide and confidant for three books. He has been a great companion over the past fourteen years.

This brings me to my five daughters. Sara has been there for the whole teaching adventure, from Purdue to Brigham Young University to Morgan Stanley and finally to HBS. She has observed and occasionally commented on my moods after great teaching and poor teaching as well. Catharine has been drawn to the classroom and has shown over time her natural gifts as a teacher. Joanna and I shared an office for two years while she studied here at HBS. She has always had the confidence to share her insights about my teaching style. Jayalakshmi has begun to be an astute critic of her own teachers in school. Devika simply believes in me regardless of my abilities as father or teacher. An honorary member of our family is Haydee Garcia. I have gratitude and admiration for how she has helped raise our kids.

Finally, Vineeta has a way of supporting and challenging my work and helping articulate my creative intent. She has tried to refine my writing and ways of thinking. She sets the standard for both. Vineeta, thank you for being such an inspiration and partner.

ABOUT THE AUTHOR

Thomas J. DeLong is a Baker Foundation Professor of Management Practice in the Organizational Behavior unit at Harvard Business School.

His most recent book *Flying without a Net* was recognized by the editors of Amazon Publishing as one of the top ten books written on leadership this century.

Before joining the Harvard faculty, DeLong was chief development officer and managing director of Morgan Stanley Group, Inc., where he was responsible for the firm's human capital and focused on issues of organizational strategy and organizational change.